# girlSpoken

## from pen, brush & tongue

# girlSpoken

## from pen, brush & tongue

edited by Jessica Hein, Heather Holland, and Carol Kauppi

Second Story Press

Library and Archives Canada Cataloguing in Publication

GirlSpoken : from pen, brush & tongue / edited by Jessica Hein,
Heather Holland and Carol Kauppi.

ISBN 978-1-897187-30-2

1. Teenagers' writings, Canadian (English). 2. Teenage girls—Literary
collections. 3. Canadian literature (English)—Women authors. 4. Canadian
literature (English)—21st century. 5. Art, Canadian—21st century. I. Hein,
Jessica II. Holland, Heather III. Kauppi, Carol, 1952- IV. Title: Girlspoken.

PS8235.T43G57 2007      C810.8'092837            C2007-903517-5

Cover and text design by Melissa Kaita
Front cover photos © istockphoto.com

Printed and bound in Canada

*Second Story Press gratefully acknowledges the support of the Ontario Arts Council
and the Canada Council for the Arts for our publishing program. We acknowledge
the financial support of the Government of Canada through the Book Publishing
Industry Development Program.*

ONTARIO ARTS COUNCIL
CONSEIL DES ARTS DE L'ONTARIO

Canada Council    Conseil des Arts
for the Arts      du Canada

Published by
SECOND STORY PRESS
20 Maud Street, Suite 401
Toronto, Ontario, Canada
M5V 2M5
www.secondstorypress.ca

# acknowledgments

First and foremost, we are indebted to the contributors and to each one of the eight hundred girls who had the courage to put a letter in the mail or press SEND on an e-mail in order to share her work with us. Deciding which pieces to include in the book was arduous given the well of talent and wisdom that came our way. We feel blessed to have received so many phenomenal pieces. Thanks to each and every one of you — eight hundred times over.

We also extend much appreciation to the team of wonder women at Second Story Press: Margie Wolfe, Carolyn Jackson, Phuong Truong, Emma Rodgers, and Melissa Kaita. And to our selection committee of girls and young women from Canterbury Secondary School in Ottawa who were an invaluable part of our team: we are indebted to you for your commitment and dedication to the book project. This small crew of amazing young women offered gut reactions and thoughtful comments on a whole slew of pieces: Allison Bingham, Nina Drystek, Elena Potter, and Jessica Shewbridge.

Many thanks to faculty members, students and staff in the School of Social Work at Laurentian University for housing and supporting the project; Dr. Henri Pallard, Department of Law and Justice, Laurentian University, for countless hours of advice and encouragement; as well as the Laurentian University Faculty Association and the Canadian Association of University Teachers for providing support when it was needed. We pay tribute to Lori Scotchko for always being a part of the project in spirit; Christine Leakey, for her brilliance in designing *GirlSpoken*'s website, logo and "look"; Elizabeth Brockest and Tiina Kivinen for their contributions, including their help in getting *Making Her Mark* off the ground; Jim Hein for his help in getting the book into the hands of girls and young women; Amanda McLeod for hours of attentive listening and discussion; Susan Mather and Rachel Sutton for their thoughts and nourishment; the Women's Studies Department at the University of Guelph for their belief in the project during its humble beginnings; the Ontario Trillium Foundation for its funding of the *Girl-Spoken* project and the organizations that participated in the *GirlSpoken* Collaborative or lent support in other ways; Dr. Purnima Sundar and the School of Social Work at Carleton University for their backing and assistance; and NSCAD University, in particular, Peter Dykhuis, Tonia DiRisio and Dan O'Neill at the Anna Leonowens Gallery, Dr. Jayne Wark, Historical and Critical Studies, and Laurie Omstead, Foundation Division, for their enthusiasm and support. Thanks also to the Gallery for making possible an exhibit of the creative works in the book.

We congratulate the teachers, parents, youth leaders, service providers, librarians, and guidance counselors who encouraged girls and young women to submit their work — this book would never have come into existence without your collective enthusiasm. In particular, we give many thanks to teachers Barb Sunday and Mark Hedges, whose dedication completely exceeded our wildest hopes.

And last but not least, our thanks to our loved ones for their unfailing belief and encouragement.

# contents

**beauty:** rants & reflections on love, desire & the beauty beast

**strength:** speaking out about our struggles & calling for change

**becoming:** tales of where we've been & visions of where we're going

## conclusion: of the book, not the story

## a closer look: grounding girls' voices in a feminist approach

In purchasing this book you've
contributed to continued arts-based
work with girls and young women.

# introduction

*Brighter, Louder, Stronger*

The pages that follow demonstrate the undeniable tenacity and brilliance of girls and young women. Dozens of contributors from diverse circumstances, backgrounds, and beliefs have gripped pens and paintbrushes to tell the world what it *is* to be a girl in Canada. The poetry, prose, and art in the book is non-fictional and offers a glimpse into aspects of the contributors' thoughts and experiences. These young women are announcing that the their lives are complex and unique — through their work, they are saying, *"we are **brighter, louder, and stronger** than much of the world thinks we are"*.

When given the chance, girls and young women will name and speak and challenge. By publishing this book, we are creating a space for girls to defy the expectations and judgments that society places upon them. Many books that have been created about girls focus on their lack of self esteem, painting girls as disempowered. By inviting girls to send pieces for this book, we asked, "what are the stories of girls' lives?" and "what do these reflections of self tell us about girlhood in Canada?" Here, we strive to let girls tell their own stories, which bring to light their struggles while also revealing their strengths and their resilience.

Our contributors' experiences, emotions and opinions are clearly their own — and yet there are many commonalities in what they have to say. Again and again, in the letters accompanying their submissions, girls have told us that they want other girls to know they are not alone in what they are experiencing. Our hope is that this anthology will provide an avenue to do just that: we want this book to enable girls and young women to talk to one another by speaking in their own diverse voices about issues of importance in their lives.

*Our Story*
The first stirrings of this project grew from conversations between Jess and Heather about what it was like growing up *girl*. Having just exited our own adolescence, we were both in our early twenties and were fully immersed in Women's Studies degrees at the University of Guelph. On the living room floor of our student house, with mugs of tea in hand, we looked at our teenage years with fresh eyes and talked about what had mattered to us and what had overwhelmed us. We had honest conversations about some of the experiences of girlhood that can leave a girl's confidence in shambles. We talked about navigating the intensity of new emotions. We ranted about seeing sexism for what it is and how it had affected the ways we felt about ourselves. We questioned things we'd been told about how the world works and how we *should* be. We charted our firsts — everything from losses to kisses, growing bodies to loves.

Our own girlhoods had shared a common thread — journal pages and blank canvases had absorbed our big moments while growing up (and still do). We trusted that we weren't the only girls who found personal truths in art and writing. We wanted to create more avenues for girls to express themselves and to talk to other girls about what *is* and what *could be*. There were so many things that we wished we had heard from girls and women in our own adolescence, things we wanted to say to girls. And so we began to produce zines for girls in our community, full of both girls' work and our own writings on girlhood. We offered our first arts-based workshop at a local community centre. And then, cheering each other on, we dreamt bigger and built *GirlSpoken*, a project designed to create good spaces for girls and young women to write and paint and ramble and learn. This book is meant to be one of those spaces.

Carol joined the *GirlSpoken* team in its early beginnings as the project director. Carol has been engaged in research involving girls and young women for more than twenty years and she has taught university courses on adolescence. Being aware of the limits to knowledge and understandings about girls and girlhoods in Canada, she wanted to be part of a project that would help to fill this gap. The three of us worked together to develop a wide range of *GirlSpoken* project activities, including a survey of 556 girls and young women in Ontario, interviews with girls and service providers, and workshops for girls. Our workshops were designed to use art as a spark for discussion on topics like identity, body image, and sexuality. The art and writing that was generated in the workshops inspired us to create *Making Her Mark,* a traveling exhibit comprising some of the striking pieces you will find in this book. The exhibit got viewers thinking about what girls had to say — some realizing for the first time just how well girls can speak for themselves. It was the warm response to *Making Her Mark* that fueled the passion that has brought this book into existence.

*Our Call*
When we sent out our call for submissions, we asked girls and young women to share writing and artwork that explored their self-

expression and voice. The theme of *identity* ran as an undercurrent in the call — we asked girls what makes them who they are, what they value, and what they've experienced. We felt that if we were successful in getting our call out across Canada, and in gathering the stories of many girls, that the book would vividly contradict the popular images of girlhood that the North American mainstream media portrays. With the help of youth leaders, parents, teachers, and service providers, we got the call into high schools, homes, and drop-in centers across the country. And girls responded — over 800 of them. Our e-mail box filled and our living room floors became covered in envelopes and packages. Countless times we laughed out loud, wept in empathy, or shook with indignation as we took in the powerful messages that girls wanted to share. We were amazed at their courage and wisdom as they relayed their experiences, hopes, fears, and opinions.

Once the book project was fully underway, our team then expanded to include a selection committee of girls and young women: Allison, Nina, Elena, and Jessica. This small group of savvy girls helped nurture the book into what you are now holding in your hands.

*What's to Come*
This book is the first of its kind to combine girls' written wit and wisdom with their stunning works of art. The written pieces are a mix of journal entries, letters, short stories, poetry, and prose. The visual works are all in the form of self portraits that will offer you a glimpse into the artist's sense of self.

We have organized the creative works into broad chapter themes in order to create a dialogue between the many varied voices within the book. And yet, many of the pieces refuse to be defined and could find homes in multiple sections. We hope that as you make your way through the book, the works will begin to speak to one another throughout, and also between, the chapters. In *Voice*, contributors challenge what they're told about who they should be and articulate how they see themselves. *Beauty* is an exploration of sexuality, desire, and the messages that girls receive about what "beauty" is supposed to look like. In *Strength*, girls let you in on some of the most difficult moments of their lives — they speak honestly and call for change. The contributors in *Becoming* look back on their childhoods, describe their girlhoods, and envision who they want to be.

Throughout the book we have included results from our survey of girls across Ontario. These statistics add to the broader story and link the work in the book to other girls by showing the commonalities in the experiences and perspectives of our contributors and our survey participants. Interspersed amongst the pieces, you will also find insightful quotes from our contributors on what they want to tell the world about what it's like to be a teenage girl. In our *Conclusion*, women over nineteen share their thoughts on what *they* want to tell young women, and we also sum up some of the most salient messages the contributors want you to hear. The final section of the book, *A Closer Look*, provides more information on the *GirlSpoken* project, offers a snapshot of the book's contributors and grounds the girls' voices in feminism.

Some of the pieces that follow share an enthusiasm for girlhood that can hardly be contained by a page or a canvas; others explore its hurt, loss, or heartache. We recommend that you pay attention to the unique message within each piece, and then listen to how the contributors speak to one another. If you are a parent or if you work with girls, we trust that the truths on these pages will sound familiar. It is our intention for this book to offer you a deeper glimpse into what the girls and young women in your life are experiencing. If you are a girl, we hope that you can take something from all that the contributors are offering to you. Draw on their encouragement as you reach in to your own creativity, raise your voice, and make your way through the world.

It is our hope that this book will make its own small dent in creating change for girls and young women.

# voice

telling truths about ourselves
and our girlhoods

# voice
## telling truths about ourselves and our girlhoods

Contributors in this chapter share bold moments revealing where they've come from, who they are, and who they hope to become. Their voices are soft and strong, honest and innocent, angry and uncompromising, feisty and fierce. Many girls confront the judgments they encounter in their lives. They write about being seen as strange, odd, abnormal — they point out the ways that they don't fit in and challenge the very notion of "fitting in." Some are outraged by the barriers they face because of their gender, race, or ability. Girls also speak about the unspoken — they speak of *not* having a voice. For these contributors, putting their silence into words is a powerful act in itself.

Girls receive constraining and contradictory societal messages about their bodies, their sexualities, and women's roles. Many of the pieces reveal girls' confusion and shame as they internalize the messages they receive. They write about feeling stretched in several directions, about feeling used, about their attempts to hide their true sense of self. One contributor confesses that even the girls who appear to be confident have secrets. Girls may try to adapt to societal expectations of who they should be but, too often, these expectations aren't achievable. A few of the pieces explore the self-hatred that can surface in the face of high demands. One young woman writes about the self-harm that stemmed from her attempt to create another version of herself — she longs for the feelings of confidence she had in childhood. Yet, even with the pressure to conform, girls engage in a constant search for an understanding of the messages they receive. They search persistently and with critical minds.

Despite the anguish that comes from being told who they *should* be, girls do not ignore their own truths. They challenge societal messages, resist labels, and shape their own understandings of the world. One contributor writes about breaking through barriers, another sheds her desire to be "normal." Some, who convey sadness at being alone in their struggles, also write about their connections with loved ones. One contributor admires her mother's strength amidst her parent's separation and pledges to adapt to change and realize her full potential. A girl who feels alone also writes of knowing that she has much to offer, that she is a universe of emotion and insight. Another expresses the joy she feels in loving and being loved, a joy that sustains her when she feels misunderstood or excluded. These young women express their emotions with clarity — sadness, loneliness and fear are mixed with moments of shared joy and happiness. With paintbrushes and pens in hand, these girls boldly express who they are. And they call on other girls to do the same.

The contributors' voices are strikingly unique and yet echo each other. They are telling the world — *listen carefully. Read the layers in what we've written. See the pride in who we are. Hear us, hear our stories. See us, see our strength. And then listen again.*

# Burn a Little Brighter

Being a teenage girl is comparative to
being stretched in several different
directions. Your skin is malleable.
Physically, you are never, ever satisfied.
It's a rule. There's always something
you should be doing. Always someone else
you should be. Even the most confident of
girls have their secrets. There's no rule
book. No directions. Being a teenage girl
— it isn't paint-by-numbers. There's this
dull, aching hurt at the very centre. I'd
like the world to know that there are no
villains in this fairy tale. No sluts.
No goths punks freaks tomboys emo kids
stoners. Face the truth: we're adults,
with less of a disillusioned crust. We're
more accessible. More in touch?

If we burn a little brighter, it's
because we aren't afraid of the flame.

VANESSA FERNANDO, 15

so when do you know that you're growing up? kicking and screaming, fighting and clawing. holding paint brushes and butterfly wings in your hands, refusing to let go. i know i'm growing up because i'm starting to love myself, seeing my body as a whole rather than separate parts. a whole with light, spirituality, joy, confidence, loyalty, and love love love pouring out of it. every pore retracting and contracting with the weight of it and running and yelling like i'm a child, free from self-loathing and sadness, free to be lonely and know that it's not my fault, that i won't be lonely for long, and that with loneliness comes strength. because i am love, i am a child who has come from love, into a world that is welcoming in every tree and stone and river. i have opinions about the world and know how to express selflessness. i know i'm growing because i know it's really not about me anymore and that it never really was. it's about finding the whole, connecting the circle, creating something. so growing up is about grasping and clawing at what i believe in. bringing into me everything that will make me good and gentle... and then throwing it right back at the world because it doesn't belong to me. i can't keep the butterflies and paint brushes to myself anymore.

SARAH FERBER, 19

**Paint Brushes and Butterfly Wings**

# Me, Myself and I

BETTY HUANG, 16

# Outside Voice

I hurt / because we're imperfect.
I love / and it is joyously overwhelming.
I hate / because I need to.
I fear / failure, forgetting.
I hope / and then I'm okay.
I cry / because the tears come.
I feel / alone, so what?
I talk / but I need to shout.
I listen / yet not well enough.
I break / through barriers.
I work / for change.
I remember / simplicity.
I hold / everything within my grasp.
I hide / things under my bed things in my head.
I pray / and it's ironic.
I drive / with no gas sometimes.
I read / people horribly.
I learn / always.
I know / but second guess myself.
I sing / all the time under my breath in my mind.
I want / to soar.
I think / with my outside voice.
I am / here.
I am / still alright.


SARA SWERDLYK, 16

*We're not all super-feminist. And we're not all fluffy and pink. Being a teen girl is what you make of it, and no two girls are ever the same.*

KILEY CROSSBY, 16

ALEJANDRA PEÑA SALGUERO, 16

# Square

Behind a wall
hidden from view
This is my place
embarrassed to reveal the true me
Afraid to let go
Wish I could yell out
my secret
But fear of dagger looks
binds me
grinds me
reminds me that I'm nothing
if I'm not normal
Four corners and all sides even

OTIENA ELLWAND, 15

# more than this

What comes to mind is the heavy uncomfortable feeling of never actually believing that this is it. That this is life. Questions always remain. My confidence in the future is non-existent. Yet there must be more than this. I feel that for a long time I have been searching for passion. Something of intensity. I tried the cool image, the beautiful friends. Then there were the hard fast boyfriends and the sexual prowess. I tried self-inflicted pain through cutting, through shoving my finger down my throat. I wanted to go deeper, to find mystery in a plain and ordinary world.

Acute in my memory is the day I realized that I could be fat and undesirable. I was instantly consumed. I was never overweight, but suddenly in my eyes I was. That hurts still. Maybe it always will.

I created a hard shelled version of myself. Toward the end of school I realized that the empty feeling inside of me was not getting smaller or dimmer. Limb by limb I have climbed out of my shell. But then there was always another waiting near by. New and improved the label read. So I tried it. And found it to be just as confining. I soon discovered that instead of being made of plastic I was made of play-doh. Capable of adapting and molding myself into what I thought I was or should be.

I'm angry for women. I think I have been for some time. As a girl I was sure I was powerful. Now I despair quite easily. I look at pictures of myself. I'm confused by the golden smile of happiness I see in most. I wonder what that would feel like. The joy so easily forgotten.

RUBY VAN VLIET, 19

*Being a girl means being told who to be but never coming close enough.*

JESSICA SHEWBRIDGE, 16

# Self?

This piece represents my individuality. My face is painted to represent the aspects of myself that I conceal and the way I feel others judge me.

SHOSHANA COODIN, 17

# Through the Eyes of a Girl

I look for the deeper meaning
in everything around me.
Searching for sense in the
senseless,
and flaws in the flawless.
I try to fight the stereotypes
that place girls in the kitchen
and boys in the yard,
but I also don't resist
baking a cake
or changing a dirty diaper
or filling the role
taught to me by my mother.
I get caught up in the
expectations of others
and the ones I have for myself.
I wonder who will look
back at me
and what they'll see.

MONICA MUTALE, 14

# Untitled

JENNIFER HARESTAD, 14

# Forget Me Not

The metro doors whoosh shut and the mechanical body slowly drags itself into motion, snaking its way through the underground. Human cargo is constantly shuttled to and fro by these giants. We manage to take this luxury of transportation for granted, as so many things are taken for granted here in North American urbania. We scramble for seats and grumble about having missed the bus. We scoff at the homeless (lazy bastards), litter thoughtlessly and whine to no end when our two-hundred dollar suede Pumas get wet. Why are we, citizens of the first world, so self-centered and selfish? And what time is it anyway?

"Prochaine station, Berri-UQUAM"
My mind often spirals off on a tangent of its own, leaving utter chaos in its wake, as thoughts collide and ricochet into, through, and between one another. I haven't returned to the country in six months (the longest I've been away since I was five). I miss the land, the silence, the smell of earth, and the sap of wood, newly split. With 250 acres of land I can easily lose myself.

"Prochaine station, Champ-de-Mars"
I take in the expressions of those around me. Emotions flicker elusively across each face, remaining fixed long enough to cast a shadow or add a line. "What are they thinking?" I wonder. The observation of others has become an obsession for me, an insatiable desire to know, to understand, to feel, and to make right. I am the other and the other is me. Never fear, I'll get to the point. Society puts far too much value on directness. Truth is rarely simple. Why assume that the shortest distance between two points must always be a line? Is there no room left in our lives for the fanciful, the whimsical, the magical?

"Prochaine station, Place d'Armes"
I sit, I watch, I wait. Most of all I wonder. "Would my old friends even recognize me anymore?" I am afraid I have grown beyond my childhood... I'm not sure that it even has a place in my life anymore. When I was seven years old my parents divorced. I didn't understand it at the time but life went on. I was my mother's helper and my brother's keeper. My father has been absent from my life... but I know I loved him. He taught me about a mother's strength. He taught me that a father's love was something to be earned. My father has taught me about rejection and abandonment. He taught me that men are irresponsible and inconsistent. I took it all standing. And he left me yearning to prove otherwise.

"Prochaine station, Square-Victoria"
Where was I... ah, childhood. The events that shape us, scar us. Though memory may fail, once the pebble has been dropped the ripples inevitably continue on, reverberating through our futures, sometimes even splashing over the banks into the here and now. I often find myself on hands and knees, frantically mopping the ground in hopes of re-collecting all the precious details of past misunderstandings and betrayals.

"Prochaine station, Lucien-L'Allier"
"... yeah, well, that's because you're different," her voice rang hollow in my ears. She spoke softly, her back turned towards me as she stared steadfastly out my bedroom window. The air grew heavy with tension as I lay back on the baby pink, blue and beige tartan cover of my futon bed, refusing to acknowledge the tears that threatened to spill over my lids. Later, as she walked out the door I collapsed onto the bottom stair of our rickety staircase and lay my head in my hands. Why was I still hurting? Yes, I was different. What did I care? I was an Indian, a savage,

an Anglophone, a stranger. For awhile, I was comfortably oblivious to the white, Catholic, Francophone world outside our home. She and the others taught me how cruel children can be, towards one another and towards themselves. It hurt to have the reason for my alienation so bluntly revealed. It hurt to be separated from the rest, to be outside the boundaries of belonging. And to hear these words from the lips of my best friend was to be rejected at the most profound level of my being — betrayed, singled out and displayed for all to see. I was not and never would be like the rest. I was not and never would be accepted as one of them, not here, not now, because I was so obviously different. Because I was an oddity, an alien, a stranger in my own home-town.

"Prochaine station, Georges-Vanier"
I cannot forget, and yet I so often believe that others do. Forget about me. Who remembers the shy girl in the corner? The dark one, who you never spoke to because you knew she was different. I have such a skewed perception of myself... no... I have a skewed perception of how others perceive me. But that will change with time. As all things do.

"Prochaine station, Lionel-Groulx"
Fluorescent lights glare and I hide my face inside the folds of my sweater's black hood. Someone once said that I look like a homeless person when I'm dressed like this and maybe I do. Torn corduroys, ripped coat pockets and safety pins holding on the button, safety pins at the knees of my pants. My hands stuffed in my pockets because I didn't bother to put on gloves that morning despite the frostbite warning in effect, and shoes... well, let's not even go there. I sit on the floor of metro cars, rocking back and forth and humming to myself, enjoying the movement beneath me and the song within me. Oblivious to strange stares directed my way until someone in my company brings it to my notice — "you're so weird." I am so weird. *What the hell is that*

*supposed to mean?* "I know, isn't it great?" I laugh, but inside I'm crying again. Crying while taking public transport just isn't my thing. Am I an embarrassment to you? I've been trained to feel that way.

"Prochaine station, Place-St-Henri"
We have to adapt to change, adapt and change, allow ourselves to grow, learn from our experiences, let go and see how the bad times have helped us through, witness our own evolution, scrape off the layers of parental programming and childhood scars, reach deep down into ourselves and realize our full potential, become who we truly are. But it's so hard.

"Prochaine station, Vendome"
I stand at the last possible second, slip through the mouth of the machine and make my way up through the gray, graffiti ridden walls and cement staircases. I push onto the other side of the metallic turnstile and confront the blank sky, unwavering, my destination now within reach. Soon I'll be home.

KYRA SHAUGHNESSY, 18

## Stick with Me

It's a new year
but everything still feels the same
My life hasn't changed
I've still got bruises on my face
and a hole in my heart
I've been abused by men
and used by boys
I'm known on the streets
as a girly toy
Everyone talks behind my back
Nobody's actually been a good friend
No one's really stuck with me till the very end

But I think I've just found that someone
Someone to tell me it's going to be okay
My angel without wings

ANONYMOUS, 13

# Picnic

CHAERIM SHIN, 18

I am
I am Jessie

I am beautiful
    graceful
    enthusiastic
    silly
    helpful
    loving
    brave

I dream
I dance my emotions
My heart is filled with love
*I have*
I have Down syndrome
Something extra
A chromosome

Sometimes when people look at me
I feel that they don't see the real me
They only see some kid
with Down syndrome
Down syndrome is a big part of me
But it is not all of me
*It's not all of me*

I love to laugh
    to write stories
    to dance and sing
    to be with friends

And I love people
Be happy
for who you are in your heart
That is true!

People with Down syndrome
should be
allowed in schools
They should be treated equally
– equally
in their hearts

Sometimes people don't
understand me
At all
Sometimes I do not fit in
At school sometimes people
treat me badly
They see a girl
who has Down syndrome
They do not see who I really am

My personal feelings are:
Be gentle, do not fight
And fight for your rights!

I am Jessie
*I have*
I have Down syndrome
I have emotions and laughter
And people who love me
I give my gifts
I give my beautiful thoughts
I give lovely dreams

Come, share with me
My dreams
Your thoughts
Together we will
Change the world

JESSIE DENISE HUGGETT, 17

# My Dance

# In My Heart I Feel...

YEON SON, 17

# spin, spin stories

I am the daughter of an artist, of a mountain climber. I press dried flowers and I spin, spin stories. Sometimes I grin just because.

I'm not innocent. I'm a bitch, a rebel full of ideas. And sometimes I'm afraid. I am loved, breaking, searching. I am wild, barefooted and longing for a kiss. I breathe in cold air. I am Russian, an immigrant, a refugee. And I will never forget. I am obsessed, disturbed and searching for adventure. I am filled with doubt. I am paranoid like my mother and I'm scared of the dark. I mouth words to the air and fish for inspiration. I am tingling with expectation.

I am a future mother. I am a tea addict. I'm a cookie cutter. I am malleable like dough. And I'm surrounded by corruption. Yet, I stand on a bridge, never broken. Like my father, I am silent — despite it all. I reach out, reach in. I linger, clinging in desperation. I am trying to understand. I run my hands through water. I am lonely. I am overjoyed. Maybe I'm trying to change.

OLIA KOPOSOVA, 17

31% of girls and young women express themselves by writing poetry or stories

29% of girls and young women express themselves by painting or drawing

# into me

I stretch out long fingers of curiosity
into the luminous caverns of my mind
Hear the music that flows through my body
frightening and fascinating
I wrap long tendrils of love
caressing the scars
noting the hate
soothing the torn
encouraging the afraid
I seek daring and delight
courage and confidence
Create my own space
I soar from my cage of self consciousness
Higher and higher
Into the sky
Into the sun
Into me

RANDI EDMUNDSON, 14

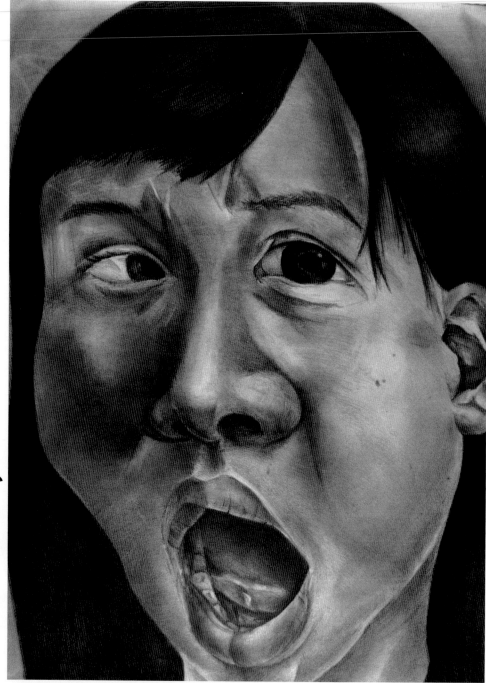

**Real Side of Myself**

# Vacancy

I welcome you to nestle in my brain.

Beneath curly red hair and a chafed and screaming skull I am trying to find solid ground. I feel hollow, scooped out, sewn crooked, strange. I'm scared and I'm exhausted, trying to hold myself together. Life bruises in subtle ways.

Outside alone there is no one to bother me, no one trying to understand, no one who wants me for another trophy. Sometimes it seems whether its solitude and quiet or music and strangers, either way, I'm lost in a crowd.

And all the while I'm wanting — hear me, hear my stories. Listen like rain listens. I am a universe. Paper without margins. An infinity of flavours. And a hunger that runs through to your toes. If wisdom is knowing — deep and guttural, a physical thirst — then the most important people are the believers and the storytellers. Those who make the ride a little easier to bear.

VANESSA FERNANDO, 15

# Unsaid

You sighed
Tap
      Slap
Drummed
Along        the        table
Tap
      Slap
You looked at me
      The table
          The floor
Tap
      Slap
You have something to say
I know
      And
I know          Say it
You won't
Tap
      Slap
Silence
      And your drumming hands
Silence
      And no words

MARTHA HARBELL, 17

# MOM

I wonder if you're safe
And have a place to stay
I wonder what you're doing
Each and every day
I wonder if you miss me
Or think of me at all
I wonder why you don't write me
Or even give me a call
I wonder if you're happy
With the choice you make each day
I wonder why you left us
And went so far away
I wonder where you are
And if you're there to stay

DANIELLE KING, 15

## Lies like Truths

She's told she's not talented enough
She's told she's not smart enough
She's told she's not strong enough

# She tries to forget
# (she's just a woman)

KATIE LOVETT, 14

60% of girls and young women are interested in learning more about or working on women's rights

# My Identity

My identity is a Black Canadian who is Jewish but discriminated against.

SHERRI MACDONALD, 13

13% of girls and young women feel like they have no one to talk to when they're upset

# Show me

When I say I don't want to talk,
encourage me to open up.
When I say I just want to die,
I'm saying I'm too scared to go on.

When I say it's hopeless,
please know that I'm tired of trying.
When I say I don't want to be touched,
hold me until I stop crying.

When I say I'm fine,
protect me from myself,
'cause that's not what I mean.

When I say no one cares,
show me that I'm wrong.

NELLIE, 14

This is how I see myself. I like things that are logical, tangible, and make sense. I always tell the truth and expect that everyone else does the same. I usually say exactly what's on my mind and it's only afterwards that my brain catches up with my tongue. I try to find beauty and good in everyone and strive always to be fair. I like to make a note of what colour the sky is. I'm often mothering, and I try to protect everyone I care about from harm. I have firm, unyielding morals — and I uphold them completely. I will stop what I am working on if my cat wants to cuddle with me. I always do my best, and insist upon perfection. I despise weakness in myself. Words are my weapons, my tongue, my sword. I belong to this earth. I flourish in my native soil and I will never leave. Dance is woven into my every step, music permeates my voice, and water supports my soul.

## my tongue, my sword

JULIA MASTRANGELO, 15

# beauty

rants & reflections on love,
desire & the beauty beast

# beauty
## rants & reflections on love, desire & the beauty beast

This chapter is full of daring submissions on desire, beauty, and self-confidence. In the pages that follow young women explore beauty from many different angles. Girls write about everything from first kisses to gender stereotypes, from masturbation to critiques of mainstream magazines. They write about the complexity of becoming a woman, understanding their developing sexualities, and confronting sexism. In their self-portraits, girls express their own visions of beauty as well as their struggles with what they're *told* about beauty.

Even our youngest contributors are fully aware of what the stick-thin image of beauty looks like. Well before their own breasts have fully arrived many girls are already anxious about having the "perfect" body. And yet the pieces in this chapter show us that girls are challenging many of the ideas about beauty that are tossed their way. Young women tackle the beauty beast by strongly defending *real* beauty. One girl confidently dismisses the idea of the "perfect" body, saying that it is impossible to obtain naturally. Another is angered by the drunken catcalls and pickup lines that evaluate how beautiful she is and suggest her place in the world. Yet another asks for her fragile and truthful message to be shared — she wants us to know that beauty is about the way we carry ourselves, it is in our kindness, our generosity, our passion.

Through their writings, girls also invite readers into their love lives — into the sweet moments and sad moments of anticipation and heartache, fear and fragility. Some girls challenge what they've been told about *who* they should desire by gently and boldly loving other young women. Many girls express their struggles in finding a balance between getting lost in love and remaining rooted in themselves. In a journal entry, a young woman explores the experience of waiting and wanting to be struck by love, even knowing that it might be painful, might wrench her heart. Through her online blog, another girl navigates the mix of eagerness and nervousness brought on by her first kisses. With startling clarity, the contributors explore the excitement, joy, and anguish of their first experiences of love and desire.

The writings and images in this chapter are rich with emotional intensity. Works delve into the interconnections between beauty and the body, desire and sexism, confidence and love. These girls and young women are wise. They know how complicated these topics are and they confront them head on. They continually call on girl readers to question what they've been told. *It's okay to make your own rules and narrate your own story. See your own beauty (trust us, you are beautiful). And love yourself in a way that shows others how to love you.*

# The Baths

we took our clothes off
got into the bath together
took turns under the faucet
to wet our hair
so we could sculpt it with
all sorts of delicious shampoos
we would stand under the shower
like it was raining
would laugh like we'd been quiet for days
the water splashing
into our mouths

we traded soap

I marveled at your breasts, your muscled thighs
you understood my nudity
took it all in
we were ourselves and each other
naked, not yet women
warmed by water
that turned cold before we were
ready for rinsing

JENN COLE, 19

49

# December 8<sup>th</sup>

This is life. Leaving me behind at shows and in the basements of my best friends. Hair dye and image problems. Love and lust. Giving in and giving up. We always look good — and if we don't it never really matters anyway because we never *feel* any different. I want these days to last forever. I want the lack of self-confidence to stay because otherwise I won't love it as much when he tells me I'm beautiful.

EMMA RUTH, 15

*Teen girls today are incredibly pressured to conform to a stereotype of beauty. Intelligence, rather than beauty, should be valued.*

JOANNE CAVE, 13

*Being a teenage girl is confusing. We have so many advertisements bombarding us everyday and it's hard not to get swept up in them. 'You're fat, lose weight, you smell, wear deodorant, you're not cool unless you're wearing...' To overcome these expectations, and see through them, is empowering.*

CAITLIN HUTT, 18

*All girls are different and that's what makes us who we are. The media pretends to understand our problems but doesn't really understand.*

OTIENA ELLWAND, 15

# I saw myself

I told him age is a state of mind,
but really, I was out of my depth

walking the streets
crossing limits and boundaries
feeling years older, feet taller
I saw myself in every girl
who gives herself away
while hoping to God the rubber doesn't break
who makes the mistake of falling in trust with the right guys
who turn out to be the wrong guys to love
in reality these first times aren't so sweet
they all seem to reek of the fishy tales
seen on the shows and shores of Dawson's Creek

sometimes I think as girls we're taught to accept
whatever it is we get —
the guys with pick-up lines and pick-up trucks
sweet-talking or cat-calling
depending on how much they've have had to drink
and from this, we're supposed to know:
we're beautiful
we're ugly
and that the world really cares what we think

ADÈLE BARCLAY, 18

# Untitled

SUMIKO SAKIYAMA, 13

50% of girls and young women want to learn more about boy-girl sex

12% want to learn more about girl-girl sex

61% said that they know someone who has had a crush on a person of the same gender

Snapshots

## sept 16

I think I have a disease. It's called the inability to like queer girls disorder. ITLQGD for short. It is diagnosed after an extended period of time where the patient has crushes only on straight girls and begins to think that the only *real* action she's ever going to get is in her imagination. My friends and I are almost all single. The difference is, they go around talking about "ex's" and I should be so lucky. I never imagined myself wanting a break up but I guess it's no different than flat-chested, naive twelve year olds wanting their period like it's some sort of currency. They whine and complain about not being able to use tampons while what they're really whining about is their desire to grow up, reach a milestone, be mature, be respected and become normal, functional, complicated teenagers. Not that I'm putting down the depth and experience of twelve year olds, but they will figuratively piss their little minds out when their wishes come true and they have to deal with the female reproductive cycle for five fucking days a month until they're fifty. See? This is me. And this is what

I'll be thinking of myself after I yell or cry my final goodbyes and go stomping out of a house/apartment/dorm room/restaurant/hallway creating mental voodoo dolls of the irritating girl I can't stand anymore. Come on love town, spread for me, let me see your face, let me feel your pain.

## sept 28

Cosmo Magazine makes me feel like a guy. Fine. It makes me feel like the stereotypical image of the conventional male — since, of course, gender is a social construct and does not actually exist. You see, I read the magazine for comic relief. In my opinion it's written for the upper-middle class, white, protestant, highly socially centered, commercially vulnerable, straight women of officially twenty to forty but actually fifteen to thirty tops. It occasionally alerts me to the testosterone running through my blood. One time I read this article telling young women what to do about men's oblivion to a woman's clothing and shoes and hairstyle. Now wait. I can never remember clothes or shoes. So take that Cosmo. That's right. I can never remember shoes and I undress girls with my mind. And I don't believe manipulative ads for belly flattening cream either. I think if it were up to Cosmo, I'd be a boy. Maybe I am.

## oct 04

As for feminism, I don't quite know what to think about it all — sure, I nail anyone I hear making a sexist comment, send out emails condemning female exploitation, or make points of refusing to do little things (like touching the left tit on Juliette's statue in Verona). 'Cause I think it is the little things that are holding up the sexist foundations in our society. But I don't spell woman with a 'y' or say 'herstory' or any of that shit, 'cause (no offence) but I think there is a line between little things that matter and stupid things that make the feminist movement look like a bunch of angry women who don't know what they're doing. Don't get me wrong, I'm the first to say that language is vital and that its subtleties form the base of its culture, but I think that trying to say things like *herstory* and *womyn* are useless 'cause the fucking word doesn't change. We should be using the words for our cause instead of wasting our time altering their spelling. I respect a woman who can make me look at a word differently by writing about it, preaching it, or singing it. I respect a woman who knows how to use a word to her advantage. Making something work for you that is already there is often more impressive than having to change it to make it work. But then, maybe the world is so caked over with men that it *needs to be changed* in order to make it work.

ROSHAYA RODNESS, 17

*Teenage girls are often thought of as worry-free, talkative shopaholics who only think about meeting hot guys. But not all girls are like that. Girls think about the world and society and worry just like other citizens.*

CHRISTINE HYUN A KIM, 17

# Untitled

CINDY LEE, 17

# This is How to be Beautiful

The image required to be beautiful

has evolved

into recession

Men once aroused by curves

hips wide enough to bear a child

Now notice a woman

who could not exist naturally

infantilized
objectified

Measured perfection cuts her in half

JESSICA SHEWBRIDGE, 16

# $3.75 for a new you

"Top 10 Signs He's Interested", "100 Ways to Look Pretty", "Cutest Spring Styles!" With these degrading messages ringing in the ears of teenage girls, no doubt that there is a drastic plummeting in self esteem and self confidence. As teenage girls, we are struggling with maintaining our self esteem and confidence while being pressured into a stick-thin reflection of beauty. The stereotype of beauty hangs over our heads like a looming thundercloud. For too long, female humanitarians, doctors, politicians and mothers have been ignored. We long to have those sunshiny, giggly girlhood days back again, when making the soccer team was our biggest concern. Our passions, dreams, and aspirations get left behind in a tear-stained diary. Too often, adolescence is about little more than popularity, vomiting up this morning's breakfast in the school bathroom, and feeling that sunken, plummeting feeling in your stomach when your crush averts his eyes.

Becoming a teenage girl is an identity-shattering process.

In truth, a beautiful individual is one who is confident, kind, motivated, intelligent, loving and passionate. Now, if only someone could whisper this fragile, truthful message into the minds of teenage girls.

JOANNE CAVE, 13

38% of girls and young women said they spend a lot of time thinking about the way they look

49% said they think that magazines, TV, and the media have greatly affected the way they think about their bodies

# Untitled

ALEXIS ARMSTRONG, 16

# All in the Frozen Afternoon

walking
> Cars on the street
> Faster than the speed of...
> Turning white snow into muck

> *Are you cold?*
> *(of course you're not)*
> *...but does she make you warm again?*

waiting
> At your bus stop
> For your bus
> For it not to come
> For you to stay with me
> And the sounds will rush past us
> And I'll pretend it's not like it is
> And you can think I'm over it
> And the promises of *maybe* will keep me guessing

wondering
> If you know
> If I want
> If you've realized
> If I should

when
> Your bus comes
> We'll hug and
> Suddenly it's all hushed
> And it's just us
> > — for a second.

[shhh.]

JULIA C. REES, 16

67

## Love Diary

### february 4

Okay. So this is weird. My leg hurts. David was just here and we were sitting next to each other, pretty close. And his arm was on my leg, just resting on my leg — nothing kinky. But now my leg is all tingly inside.

He called me cute and said I was smart and creative and other stuff. It's going really well. The awkward silence has gotten a lot less awkward now that we've both acknowledged it. And I'm a lot less uptight about everything. You know, more natural. We're both cracking jokes and laughing and just having a good time. It feels really great — I haven't felt this great in a long time.

### february 16

I got my first kiss today!!! And it wasn't even a big deal either. David and I were both freaking out about it at the time but now it's not so bad. It was a lot wetter than I thought it would be. But it was nice. I don't remember if I had my eyes open or closed. I think they were open though because I remember looking into his eyes for about a millisecond before I got embarrassed and pulled away. I didn't have my glasses on 'cause I figured that would make things weird. And I kissed him on the cheek when we had calmed down and stopped laughing from embarrassment and stuff. That was sort of awkward, but oh well.

## march 2

I was glad when David and I started kissing. It was really enjoyable, only now...now I don't know if this is right anymore. He started adding tongue the other day. I don't want to mess anything up, he's such a sweet and gentle guy otherwise. And I mean, it's not even such a big deal, right? Just a little tongue. Logically, there's nothing wrong with that. It's just another form of kissing. But we've been doing *a lot* of kissing. And when I ask him to stop, he does, but only after a little while. He says he's just acting on impulse and that makes me really afraid. I don't want his impulses to lead us into something impulsive, you know?

## march 4

You know, all this kissing makes me feel really special. Like finally I'm good enough for someone to want me. And that someone is a really good guy too. He's funny and sweet and handsome and just really good. I don't want to lose him. But I don't want to lose myself either.

CAITLIN OLESON, 15

26% of girls
and young
women want
to learn more
about sexual
consent

# The Behind of a Peacock and I

I was inspired by the reflection of the face I see in every reflective surface no matter where I go.

ZANN HEMPHILL, 16

# **dancing** naked

*I'm Happy*
I'm walking home from school and I realize there's candy left in my pocket.
I'm lying on the bunk of Maija's cabin — we're deciding which guys we'd sleep with.
I'm riding home from Greg's on our two-month, watching the moon rise. He wraps me in his arms and whispers "I love you".

*I'm at Peace*
I'm alone in my room with all my candles lit. I can't hear anything but my music.
I'm canoeing through Frontenac Park, in perfect stride with Derek.
I'm lying on a beach watching the stars, with Ben as my pillow.

*I'm Alive*
I'm dancing naked in a public fountain at two o'clock in the morning.
I'm sneaking out of my dorm room and down two flights of stairs.
I'm leaping from a cliff into a clear blue lake, my boyfriend's swim shorts clutched tightly in my left hand.

*I'm Me*
I'm at a punk show when a 30 year-old man shoves me forwards. I turn around and shove him back.
I'm skiing backwards down an icy hill because it's snowing and I can't find my ski goggles.
I'm running across the street in -40 degree weather with no coat on. Barefoot.

KAT SALMON, 16

# Untitled

HILARY PARK, 18

# In My Head

I buy cigarettes
purchase them secretively
and the store clerk
takes no notice of my age
I ask the young guy in a leather jacket for a light
and we stroll down the street

I wear short skirts
dye my hair black
and piercings adorn me
Though I can't help but add
pink frills and bright eyes

I fight, kiss, retort, don't give a damn
don't want what I can't have
and get what I want
I do these things I've never done
And I don't need to
because I've already done them
In my head

CLAIRE HEISLER, 17

I fight, kiss, retort

# Lost

You pinned a veil
Over my innocence
With weak story lines
And a charming smile

My virginity is lost
In your emptiness
Like a gem
Out of sight
At the absolute bottom
Of a well
Where wishes are rejected

AMY MURPHY, 17

# Surgery

the fern you gave me
sits on my t.v. tray
next to the tylenol 3

the fern you gave me
is painfully fragile and
sinfully tiny
and it flutters
next to my witty remarks
and incidental compliments

and I wish I could say it was the drugs
and I wish I could say it was the drugs
and I wish I could say it was the drugs

you're charming
please keep me in sunlight
and stop me from getting dry

KAITLIN SCHWAN, 18

# To Shave or Not to Shave

To shave or not to shave, that is the question.
Whether tis nobler in a leg to suffer
The cuts and scratches of outrageous fashion,
Or to take arms against a sea of smoothness
And by opposing, ignore it and let it grow.
To shave no more, but by a shave to say
We end the thousand petty jibes that hair is heir to.
Tis a situation easily avoided.
To shave, to shave perhaps to fit in. Ay there's the rub,
For in not fitting, what tests may come,
When we've admitted that it matters much,
May give us pause.
For who would bear the looks and scorns of society?
Th'eyebrow raised, the jerkwads' passing jest,
The pangs of changeroom comparisons, and the spurns of
undermining thoughts.
This is when she herself might her surrender make with a bare calf.
It is the dread of submission that may make us rather bear this fur
we have
Than fly to standards smooth.
Yet fuzziness does make outcasts of us all.
And thus my ardent resolution
Is sicklied o'er with the cast of a silky thought
And I enterprise quick to remove it.
Thus I lose the name of activist.
Oh, how soft you now!
Be all my intents remember'd.


AVELYN WALDMAN, 14

59% of girls and young women
are interested in learning more
about body image

# Rose Like Day

YO OUN CHOI, 17

# Open Letter

To sisters, strangers, and friends:

I was born in the Philippines eighteen years ago. The same year the anti-depressant Prozac was introduced. It's ironic, the introduction of Prozac and my first breath — like the world knew depression and I were going to meet.

At the age of one my father died. After his death, my mother went abroad to go to school and I was left in the care of my grandparents. I have two pictures of my dad. One is of him holding me on my first birthday. He looks like a nice man. The second one is a headshot — his and mine. Him smiling, me smiling.

At the age of three I remember being at the airport, crying. I was leaving for Canada with my mother and saying goodbye to my grandparents. I remember trying to run away from my mother. My grandparents were my family and my mother was a stranger. But I had to go with her — a new family and a new country. The first couple of years in Canada were challenging for me and my mom. We lived in a rough neighbourhood housing complex and my mother desperately ran around trying to find a stable job. She protected me from many of the challenges and for the most part I was a content kid.

At the age of eight I was the flower girl at my mother's wedding. I hated her husband and felt like he tried to buy my love through chocolates and stuffed animals. I was happy without a father-figure. I thought we were fine — just my mom and me. Really, I was afraid he would replace me.

At the age of ten I started the whole puberty stage. I read *Are you there God? It's me Margaret* by Judy Blume. She talked about breasts, boys, menstruation, and the whole deal. My friends and I thought it was funny, but deep down we all knew it was going to hit us.

At the age of eleven I got my period. I became a "woman." Who exactly defines "woman" anyway? It's funny how the use of a maxi pad does. At eleven, I also went to my first boy-girl party where I tried smoking cigarettes for the first time. I thought I looked attractive with a cigarette. I remember painting a pencil with white out (to make it look like a cigarette) and pretending to smoke in front of the mirror. That was the same year I started to masturbate. At first I wasn't sure if it was okay for me to do or not, since I grew up as a Catholic believer. Magazines said it was healthy to explore your body whereas my church viewed it as a taboo, a sin. I still did it, regardless. Sometimes I felt ashamed and other times I just didn't care.

That same year I became an older sister. It was also the same year that my grandfather died. After that, I stopped caring about anything.

At the age of fifteen my best friend got a boyfriend and I felt like I had no one. Then one night I met some guy in a chat room on the internet. Internet conversations soon became phone conversations. Most days I could hardly stay awake at school after talking with him all night. He was the first guy I ever said *I love you* to. One day we decided to meet in a public place, and I realized I didn't really know him and I didn't really love him. So I dumped him and he called me a cold heartless bitch. He made me feel like shit. He said I ruined him. He said I was the reason he became suicidal. I began to blame myself, question myself, hate myself for what I did to him.

That same year I developed an eating disorder. I don't really know how it started. I wanted the twiggy model look. To me, that was beautiful. I would starve myself on a daily water diet. Sometimes if I felt like it, I would eat a cracker. The weapon I used on my body was a toothbrush.

In a way, she was my best friend, my magic wand. It wasn't even a food thing — I hated myself and throwing up what was in me made me feel like I was throwing away my internal self.

That was the same year I experimented with marijuana. I loved it. I remember going to class stoned and having the time of my life. And then I would come off it, and life would feel inevitably far worse than actual reality.

At the age of sixteen, I fell in love with my first boyfriend. I remember getting all red and feeling a million butterflies in my stomach. The butterflies were the best part. And the way he kissed me — unexplainable. He was the first guy I felt really comfortable with and he helped me to see myself as beautiful. The whole time we were together I thought about having sex with him but I wasn't sure and I feared pregnancy.

At the age of eighteen, I'm trying now to be friends with who I am. I'm no longer anorexic, bulimic or depressed, but sometimes I can still feel it's a part of me. I have a lot of sadness in my life, but I've also gained optimism. The world has so much to offer me...I can feel it. I'm actually excited for life.

There's so much more to me than these words, but they're all I can share with you. I hope you find comfort in them.

Yours,

*Diana*

DIANA BIACORA, 18

# Orangeinfinity

I
the sunset feels like it goes on forever and
i kick my feet to bring the swing higher away
from the sand [gritty sand] digging into the
skin on my feet and hands and when i swing this
high i feel like i'm in kindergarten except
i'm too tall and i'm wearing punk bracelets
with skulls and my eyes are lined in neon pink
and black and my fingernails are bitten and
bitter from purple nailpolish and my jeans and
t-shirt show a little too much skin for a five
year old's innocence

II
at night we sit in the parking lot of dq's and
eat ice-cream [i think i've fallen in love
with drive thrus and strawberry sundaes and
the people who bring me here] and we play the
music too loud like the time i rode with a
boy — a boy who can't see himself in my eyes
and sometimes i'm afraid he never will and
then next year he'll be in college and i'll
never get the chance to say anything but i'm
too afraid because there's this person in the
way, his girlfriend [i hate this sometimes]
but we did drive down the highway and i put
my feet on the dash and sang along to music

i didn't know anything about and the windows
were shaking and so was i when he joked about
the back seat and didn't see me blush

III
i feel like i'm sleepwalking most days because
nothing in life has ever felt this good, like
pure and sunshine… i just feel like something
that's intangible and untouchable and i've
noticed that i don't flinch quite as much when
people brush up against me and when he leans
on my shoulder i [almost] want him to keep
his hand there so that i can remember the way
he rubs his nose when he's tired or bored and
how his face changes when he sees me [bored
to shining smile and i wish that i knew that
it was **me** who made him smile] and how the
leather of his motorcycle jacket smells or
how he holds my hand a second too long when he
helps me stand [i wish i knew that he did it
on purpose] or his jokes or the way he runs
his fingers through his hair and i swear that
i'm not obsessed i'm infatuated and why is
everything always about a boy?


ERIN LORENZ, 16

## Boy

Us. We're in my bedroom. Silent enough to hear footsteps coming up the stairs. So we communicate through eye contact and smiles. The kind of smiles you don't see, but you can feel against your neck. His hands look as soft as they feel. The street lamps shining through the window leave a blue tinge on his skin, making me so grateful to touch him and watch the way his expression changes as the night carries on. And under my breath, close to his ear so he can just make out what I'm saying, I whisper, *I wouldn't have it any other way.*

ANONYMOUS, 15

all about me JAE-YOUNG HWANG, 18

# Written After Band Camp

I talked for hours
with the hazel-eyed girl
sitting on a camp mattress
between sleeping bags and pillows
with Miles Davis on in the background

I watched her and her sketchbook
as she drew

                        an intricate pattern

a spiders            e
      w                    b

now, not then,
I knew
if she had a web
I'd be the fly
                [her fly]
drawn to silk web
                [silky skin]
she'd    bind me
          wind me
          twine me
          kind-a like me

I wonder if she'd
          suck me
                dry
if I were the fly...

she stared out the window
and I stared with her
on a bus rolling by
watch the night
feel it breathe

      "I don't want to go home"
      "Neither do I"

JULIA C. REES, 16

# Womanhood

Past the sacred protective
nest of golden childhood,
womanhood was
something thrown at me
when I was unaware and
looking elsewhere.
To the teases and jeers of
my classmates,
I clumsily caught it and
flaunted it unknowingly
with its enticing tassels of
freedom and sexuality.

BERTHA WONG, 19

# loving it!

It's not
often that
a girl loves
her body
and mind.
I consider
myself to be
strong and I
like to inspire
other girls
and young
women
to love
themselves.

YEKATERINA
YELIZAROV,
17

# strength

speaking out about our
struggles & calling for change

# strength

## speaking out about our struggles & calling for change

Girls' resilience is the foundation of this chapter. Here, young women frankly depict their burdens and show how they cope in spite of the pain they carry. For some, their strength lies in the act of capturing difficult words and images on paper. They bravely portray their isolation and abandonment, self-hatred and self-healing. Many of the contributors show how they've been able to forge a strong sense of self in the face of adversity. The pieces show how life's challenges sometimes hit with blunt force but girls draw on their strengths to cope, heal, and thrive. These pieces are powerful and you may carry some of them with you for awhile. This is likely what these young women intended — for girl readers to hold a reminder that they are not alone.

One of our contributors claims that girls' lives are much too complicated to be summed up in pieces of poetry. While she is most certainly right, these works *do* manage to let you in on some of the most salient aspects of girls' lives. They straightforwardly write and paint about discrimination, bullying, depression, abuse, and harassment. Their works convey some of the intensity of their experiences in a way that hits home, stimulates thought, and hopefully, provokes change.

These young women call for change in everything from anti-bullying programs to the inclusion of youth voices in places that matter, from a re-telling of history to a world that is free of abuse and discrimination. Some contributors beckon girl readers to rely on other girls and women as they work towards creating change. In her poetry, one contributor thanks women in her life for their inspiration, and calls on all women to stand strong, be proud, and draw on each other's wisdom. In tandem, many girls offer their own shoulders and lives to lean on because they desperately want girls to know that other girls understand.

The pieces in this chapter also reveal that girls *cope* in many different ways. A few of these contributors write about using creativity as a means for learning, understanding, and self-healing. Through the solace of nature, a young woman finds release. In music, one girl finds compassion and the beginnings of recovery. Another tells us that she, herself, is the only one she can really count on for understanding. A few of these young women turn to cutting, others to their drugs of choice. With insight and self-awareness, they write about their experiences of struggle and survival.

The strong girls and young women, whose pieces have found a home in this chapter offer up, not only their challenges, but also their visions for change. *With strength and courage, we can reach in to heal and reach out to bring about change. We have rights and must demand them — because we have so much to offer the world.*

# I am Woman

"I was loneliest when I was married."
–52-year-old alcoholic

"I know that I've fucked up as a mother."
–48-year-old overachiever

"He abused me. Not bad or anything,
but I had to use cover-up on my arms
to hide the bruises."
–26 years old and finally free

"I know what I do is bad for me, but
at least I'll look good until I die at
thirty-five."
–15 years old and lost

"I remember how happy I was when I
weighed under ninety pounds."
–43-year-old perfectionist

"I'm fairly certain he was sleeping with
her when we were together."
–18 years old and finding herself

I am woman. Hear me roar.
But hang on just one second,
I have to apply some lip-gloss and fix my hair.

How do I look, sir?
Do you approve?

Am I fuckable?
Do I turn you on?

We are so many things,
with so much more to offer
than what we allow ourselves to show.

It wouldn't be very ladylike of us to hold our own door open.
Now, sit up straight and cover your mouth when you cough.
Smile with your teeth (not your gums) and suck in your gut.

We're tiptoeing through this world,
watching our steps so as not to disturb.
We're joining the ocean of expectations,
and we're sinking like stones.
Applying red nail polish, I cover the imperfections
with the bloodshed of all those women
who sacrificed themselves for the right
to be a woman in man's clothing.

Our stomachs scream for change.
We kneel over toilets and plunge our fingers down our throats,
to gain control, to purge our frustrations,
throwing-up everything that really matters
for everything that doesn't.

Ashamed of my hypocrisy,
I'm screaming as loud as I can,
but my own hand covers my mouth.
I complain about my thighs, my ass, my nose, and apply make-up daily.
I'm running out of air. It's getting cold and dark in here.
So I'm begging you to please
illuminate me with your experience,

and teach me how to fly.
My wings are rusty, but it's my turn
to leave the nest and all the rest
to glide alone.

So come on, girls, let's fight.
It's not over yet.
To every female doctor, lawyer, priest and mother,
I bow my head and thank you for the inspiration.
Talk to me, women.
I'm ready and willing to listen.
Don't be ashamed of your age,
be proud of your wisdom.
Because you, me, she
are choking on magazine advertisements.
We're being poisoned by the ink
that sinks into our bodies,
that's programming us with
"21 ways to please your man" & "15 steps to a firmer stomach".

To all women with whom I've been blessed to converse,
I say this:
there is hope. It's never too late.
If you just open your eyes and see
that we
have so much to offer this world —
you and me.
For, I am woman. Hear me roar
(as I sneak into the bathroom
and kneel on the floor).

CAITLIN HUTT, 18

*Girls can survive anything. And rarely escape any stage of life unscathed. The trick is to enjoy it — fill your life with wonder. Notice your spirit. Shut out all the voices trying to shame you and surround yourself with people who love you. Girls need other girls.*

JENN COLE, 19

# Empowered

My art tracks my progress, my learning, my emotions — who I am. As a young woman, it is hard to be comfortable in your body and feel confident in who you are. This piece is about finding strength while living in a patriarchal culture. It represents the incredible spirit and strength that I have found in my friendships with girls and women.

SHAWNA LONDRY, 16

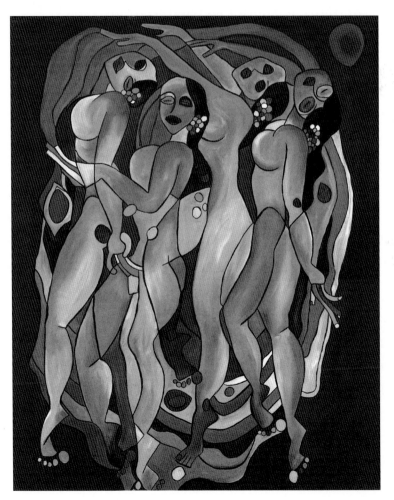

# Until Now

I'm never sure how much to share
Should I keep it all inside
Not let anyone know the real me
Not let them learn all I've tried to hide
All these years
All these years in pain
It's time to break free
And everyone will learn what my father's done
They'll finally learn about everything
I'll never be able to forgive

*"I want everyone to know that even though I live in a wealthier town, not everything is perfect about our family. My father's abuse really scarred me. And it's hard because we're trying to pay back the money he owes and he doesn't pay child support. Many kids have to go through this and I want them to know that they're not alone."*

TARRYN LEE, 14

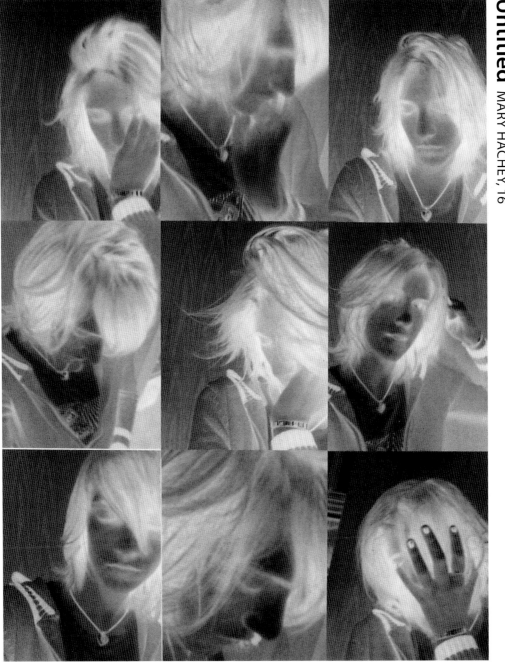

# In the eyes

To the eyes that
see me I look
normal. But I know
that ~~with~~ within
I'm The total
opicet. To the
eyes that see
me I'm smart
but I know that
within it's not
true. To the eyes
that see me
I'm happy but
I know that
inside I'm crying.
To the eyes
that see me
I'm calm but
to myself I'm
crazy.

# I want

I want to be Pretty
I want to be Smart
I want to be loved
by all.
I want to be liked
for more then just
a friend.
I want to stop
Cutting.
There's so much that
I want but dosent
feel like will
happen.

By: *[signature]*

KATIE-LYNN, 14

# Mask

This is a painting I did while I was depressed. It is representative of how I felt I was showing one face to the world, but was feeling like someone completely different underneath.

SHANNON MAY, 16

*As girls, sometimes all we need is a hug, other times all we need is space. But an 'I love you' or two can always help.*

EMILY HARRIS, 17

# Shadow of Me

dragging me over the border
of my beat
you beat
you beat it out of me
with my head against a headboard
we're at a crossroads of you and me
and I am not free
as you pound the rhythm
of me
into the wall above my head
on your bed
and I scream
silently
as you hijack me
and make me
who you want me to be
and I kiss you gladly
and bleed sadly
as you rape me
consensual definitions
break me
as you shake another
qualification of we
and rip me at the seams
and whisper through my tears
baby how do you feel?
and I crawl
tumble
fumble
my way to the door
scraping over the floor

and muffle my scream
as I cry
into a pillow case
that smells like sex
and weed
and dried up dreams
look what you did to me
you did to me
I did to me
tortured muscles
and ripped sinew
make me one
of your atrocities
broken girl doesn't know
what to do
are you through?
through with me?
set me free
I gotta set me free
so i can scream
on my field of crushed dreams
and repeat
my defeat
repeat
repeat
repeat
because sometimes
sometimes
sometimes
i liked it
when you kissed me

SARAH MCLATCHIE, 19

60% of girls and young
women have experienced
some form of harassment
or abuse

# Click, Click.

*This piece is based on the worst relationship I've ever experienced. Writing it was a form of closure for me.*

Online (ol).
Click, click.
Meet your (ur) one (1),
Your (ur) only.
Love (luv) is ('s) only
A click away.

ASL, please (plz)?
He is ('s) Chris.
17/m/alb.
"I bet you (u) sound beautiful."
Click, click.
Shut down? Click yes.

Dial ten (10) quick numbers (#z)
Click ten times (10x).

"I can't wait to (2) see ( c ) you (u),
your (ur) picture (pic) is lovely."
He has a deep voice.
Gruff and intense.

Click, click.
He pays for the (t/) bus tickets,
They're (thr) booked
Online (ol).
Thrill and anticipation for both.
Emoticon that.

Chris nowhere in sight.
But a man, not 17.
"I'm here to (2) pick you (u) up.
Chris waits at (@) home."
Hurry into the car.
Keep moving.

Late in the night (nite).
The car stops with (w/) the cold heart (h).
No one (no1) to call.
Mixed with blood, force and hurt.
Click, click.
Disconnected (dc).

CHELSEA JONES, 18

"This piece is a page from my scrapbook. My writing is both an outlet for my creative energies and a source of healing."

### Caution: I Contain...

Bottled emotions.

Chemical affirmations
and synthetic pride.

My presence will invoke panic's hand,
clasping your neck tightly,
the acid of anxiety
coating your tongue.

Hands wrought with worry,
nails shred by nerves.

### Take 2 Tablets Twice a Day with Water –

Ignore their bitter taste.
Thick and chalky.

Lethargic,
thoughts leave you

# All Women

Women — we are smart and we are beautiful

We need to follow our own paths

Be thankful for who we are

For our wisdom, our beauty, our strength

Let's speak out and take control of our lives

We have the right to be free of abuse

Because we are women and we are strong

DARCY KADLUTSIAK-DEVRIES, 15

# 66% of girls and young women are interested in learning more about racism

# New Life

My self-portrait reflects the difficulties in moving to a new country as my family and I faced racism and learned a new language.

CHRISTINE HYUN A KIM, 17

# Escape

The air is cool, all is well
Hidden in the grass
the wind chants its song to me
There is nothing to disturb me here
nothing to remind me of the pain
I have the sky as a roof
the grass as a floor
the wind as my blanket
And my good thoughts to keep me warm
I just listen to the wind chanting
its soft and graceful song

ANONYMOUS

# One with the Environment

CARMEN LEE, 16

# For Joshua

I loved being pregnant, not that I am telling anyone to go out and get pregnant, but it put a lot of things into perspective for me.

I got pregnant just after my 16th birthday. I have learned many unfortunate lessons earlier than they should ever have been taught. I was physically abused from birth to six years old. I have been involved with the Children's Aid Society since I was born. I have smoked since I was 11, drank since I was about 12, and did weed for a year. I had sex for the first time when I was 15 but it wasn't consensual. **I've realized that life isn't always easy.**

When I got pregnant, CAS moved me to a home for teen moms in a big city — that place was the best thing that ever happened to me. At the same time that I moved, my foster parents moved to the other end of the province. I was devastated. After I had my son, I only took care of him for two weeks until CAS took him out of my care, and placed him with a foster family. It was one of the staff at the home that helped me to lose my son but I am not holding any grudges. Every day since he was taken I have hated myself and blamed myself for losing Joshua. This led me to allow my foster parents to adopt him. And now I'm here without my son.

I've learned a lot. I followed the path that made the most sense to me. To those who have been there and supported me... I will NEVER EVER EVER EVER forget you.

ANONYMOUS, 16

# The Potter

Rusty water

From nail bed to elbow

A potter with rag-like hair

A single mom

Never looked stronger

AMY MURPHY, 17

117

# She Inspires Me

She is the wind — always by my side — supporting me, pushing me forward.

I am a book with too many words, too many sentences, too many thoughts. Yet she opens me calmly and with perfect care puts every word, every letter, and every comma in its rightful place. She helps me to see my true self and find my strengths. She shows me the importance of cracking open my spine and allowing the world to read with me. She teaches me how to be a mirror to others, helping them to see their true, amazing selves.

I am so lucky to have found her. All I had to do is look within. And I know that she is within each of us. She is whispering in our thoughts, pushing us from behind. Listen to her. Lean on her.

*"I've always felt somewhat alone in my struggles, like no one understands me. I have found that although inspiration and support from others is wonderful, we must also look within ourselves for encouragement."*

CAYLEE RABER, 16

# Untitled

JANINE TALLIO, 17

*Young people are the solution. Don't ever listen to those who are trying to hold you back.*

ANONYMOUS, 15

# **Untitled** OLIVIA YANG, 18

# never normal

I just want to be normal
But in truth, there's no such thing

Most people think I'm able-bodied
Since I can see and breathe and walk
My mouth doesn't move how I want it to
I really hate the way I talk

I can't hear the high notes
Or whisper with my friends
I can't chat in darkness
Or even answer phones
This limits my employment
Society condones

When I miss something someone says
They look at me like I'm strange
Like reading lips
Is mine and mine alone

Raise awareness.
*Something has to change.*

JANELLE RIEDSTRA, 19

# when you're yourself

Dear Jaclyn,

You just asked me to find out for you who's going to a party you didn't even invite me to. I felt so hurt. It feels to me like you don't care about anyone but you pretend to care about everyone. Everybody pretends to love you but nobody likes you.

Getting older seemed to change everything about you. I don't know what happened that summer but whatever it was it made you want to be the best, most popular girl in school so bad that you did whatever you could to get it. And you did — **you gained popularity**. Hooray for you, but are you sure that's really what you wanted? Like, is this really all that? I'm so frustrated with you because you are such an awesome friend when you are real, but most of the time you're not. And your real personality is so great, we have so much in common — when you're yourself.

I hope my letter makes you think a little.

Hannah

HANNAH SCHULTZ-DURKACZ, 13

# Confessions of a Mean Girl

I used to be a *Mean Girl* (and I am writing this with a straight face, because it is the truth). Not as mean as the girls in the Lindsay Lohan movie, but believe me when I say that many of my fellow peers used to believe that my group of friends were the most terrifying clique in the world. Scarier than the monsters that lived under your beds from kindergarten to grade two. Scarier than the thought of eating broccoli. Even scarier than the cooties that all grade three boys spread.

My group of friends (also known as the *Purse Club* because we were the only girls in our middle school who carried purses) were plainly mean. Definition of a *Mean Girl*: a girl who mentally, physically, or emotionally terrorizes girls who are not within their social circle. So, I never physically hurt anyone, but I did cause other people to physically hurt themselves (a time in grade six that I will never instigate again). The *Purse Club* made it our mission to make fun of people who were not as "perfect" as us. Basically, our mandate was the same as other A-list cliques — spread rumours and gossip, steal people's boyfriends, insult people's clothing, the list goes on.

Now, I'll probably never know why I chose to hang out with the friends I did, and I'll probably never know why I enjoyed hurting other people and making them feel less of themselves. But I do know that as soon as I went into high school, everything changed. I was separated from the *Purse Club*. I was no longer at the top of the social scene. I was at the bottom. Grade nine was a tender year. But it was also the year that I became involved in my school and in my community, organizing dances and food drives.

Most people think that high school is the reign of the *Mean Girls*, but, in reality, it begins in grade five when suddenly everyone's starting to date and buy designer clothes. The concepts of bullying can be overanalysed until pigs fly, but the fact is, people grow out of it. I grew out of it, all my old friends grew out of it.

As a self-diagnosed *Mean Girl*, I know that teenage meanness goes away, just like many of the other symptoms of teenage life. But if you're looking for a 'meanness prevention program', involve girls in the community, in the arts, in sports. If I had had more of those kinds of opportunities then I wouldn't have been such a mean person.

YAZZY, 17

28% of girls and young women feel excluded or don't feel accepted at school

6% feel harassed or bullied

48% say that the majority of their friends would react to someone 'coming out' by saying it's okay but then avoiding the person

45% of girls and young women are interested in learning more about bullying

# Bathroom Walls

At my high school, declarations like 'for a good time call _____' or '_____ is a whore' are the daily news of the bathroom walls. What do you think when you read stuff like that? Do you believe it? Do you laugh? Do you spread the news over lunch and in the halls? Have you ever been the one with the words? Have you ever been the one on the other end?

I was the one with the pen at one point in time. But then someone wrote about me — ugly words, words that left me shaken, left me questioning myself. After I read my name, I'd ask myself, 'If I wear this shirt will I look like a slut?' or 'If I walk like **this** will they think I'm easy?' Words that go up on bathroom walls — words like bitch, slut, hoe, tramp — are difficult to argue with. They're up on the wall and the case is closed. They may just be words, but they manage to take a piece of you with them.

DEIDRA CATHCART, 16

# Shades of Hope

I have recently been through a separation in my family. My self-portrait is about how I handled it. Forgetting about everything for awhile was all I needed to feel better.

TARA WALDIE, 15

it smarts with truth

# Like Medicine

Wading knee deep in sense

Reasonable currents
ebb
Circle my ankles
I bend
taste the water
It smarts with truth
no one wants
to drink
Force it down
All you should know
and all you should do

Wading knee deep in sense
and wishing I could drown

MARTHA HARBELL, 17

# Stories of Experiment

Climb inside photographs
and be someone else
there is a
drug addict
cutting lines of cocaine
on mirrors
so the world becomes bathed
in snow sparkled
hallucinations
as the floor inverts
and you fear
the nonexistent eyes
in the walls
Climb inside photographs
and be someone else
Bad acid trip
doors that don't shut
are attacking
as your ears create
a new world inside your head
footsteps on the stairs
are hurricanes

barbiturates and alcohol
You're a real fucking upper
caffeine
to counter sleeping pills
and diet pills
so blue burning neon
in your stomach
lets you know
*things have become fragile*
*....with me*
-----you're still alive-----


SARAH MCLATCHIE, 19

20% of girls
and young
women take
drugs or
drink alcohol
when they
are upset and
feel like there
is no one they
can talk to
who would
understand

# Morning

Like many my age, I was hurting. I had been hurting all my life, and it only seemed to be getting worse. A year ago, I found a blog that encouraged youth to express themselves artistically or otherwise, and I decided to write as a way of dealing with my hurt.

As I blogged, journaled, worked through my emotions through words and poems, I found others like me. Panicked. Traumatized. Anorexic. Suicidal. Addicted. Desperate. Young. Those who interested me most were those like myself, those who injured themselves in some desperate hope to handle their grief. Cutters. All of us arranged along a continuum of self-destruction, all of us forgotten.

In my desperation I not only wrote, I began to seek music that expressed the most elusive and volatile emotions. It's so difficult to put those incomprehensible emotions to words. The reason we would rather rip our skin apart than 'talk it out' with someone is because nobody would understand. In music, I found a place where certain things make sense. I found music that made me want to see it, touch it, taste it.

Many of us lose touch with our emotions. It could be because we have been hurt too much, that we are overwhelmed with pain. When we feel this desperation we are unable to figure out what to do. Sometimes the arts can begin the cleansing of the wound. To ridicule popular music, literature or cinema that seems 'melodramatic' is to trivialize the horror many of us live everyday. Others may have considered it silly that my music was so important to me. Yet it was through this music that I was able to begin my healing.

In healing I began to push away memories. I had gotten help and once I was well I didn't want anything to do with the parts of my life that reminded me of those years. This included the music I had loved.

I recently listened to the music that had helped me. I allowed it to rend my heart again. I felt a sense of loss spread and course through me. It felt so melodramatic, so theatrical, so real. I trembled. I hurt so bad, I hurt so good, just the way I had always expected. I felt overwhelmed with the same grief, grief that I now understand.

Over this past year of healing I have come to know myself better. I know what it is to feel emotion and cope. I know that the amazing power of feeling is nothing to fear. For the first time, I can see light somewhere in this darkness. I know that I need now to say goodbye to the music that helped me find hope.

I need to feel passion, and I also know I need to feel pain. I am a conduit of pure emotion and I will never forget. I will remember my scars and I will remember those who are like me.

Through this writing, I have relived some of my hurt and pain. I'm going to bed now. Not to cut myself, I've put my blades away. I'm probably going to cry. And in the morning I know that I'll be okay.


ANONYMOUS, 19

**Anger** YO OUN CHOI, 17

# A Glimpse

*"Despite my thirty years of research into the feminine soul, I have not yet been able to answer the great question that has never been answered: What does a woman want?"*

— Sigmund Freud

Let me tell you —

Tongues and crocuses,
books and cunts,
combat boots and tutus.

Climbing the ropes after learning them,
caffeine, someone to drink it with,
a lock to keep them out, a key to let them in.

Extra-absorbent pads that don't feel like pillows,
products for us made by us,
that let us express ourselves.

History told the way we saw it go by,
spaces in places that make the decisions,
and a home without beats, kicks, black eyes or incisions.

we're handsome a

Experimenting in bed,
getting on top,
orgasms that last forever
(or at least a few minutes).
Occupations and payroll traditionally reserved for men,
the power to have organs,
that aren't named after them.

Nipple rings and dildos
we wanna drive by our own light,
and do only what feels right.

We wanna be visible, accountable, respectable, and comfortable,
cause we're handsome and wholesome and random and
girlsome,
and we're much too complicated
to be summed up in a poem.

ROSHAYA RODNESS, AGE 17

1d wholesome and

*Right now, teenage girls in Western society have more rights than ever before, and it hasn't always been this way. Remember where we came from, and keep fighting for change. Never give up!*

CHELSEA JONES, 18

# becoming

tales of where we've been &
visions of where we're going

# becoming
## tales of where we've been & visions of where we're going

In this chapter, young women consider the journey that is girlhood. They look back at their childhoods, often with nostalgia, explore what they've learned throughout their girlhoods, and discuss all that they hope to become. They write and paint about the challenges of learning to embrace their emotions and accept themselves for who they are. With honesty, many of the contributors portray their relationships with family — the complications and also the simple joys. Some express sorrow as they begin to leave the nests of childhood and come to terms with changing relationships. These pieces address the difficulties of growing, loving and leaving as girls navigate their ways into adulthood.

Many young women in this section write about their longing for the simplicity, freedom, and power of childhood. With tenderness, they explore the places and memories that have shaped their growth. One young woman reminisces about the beauty of summertime with her family and then finds, as she looks in the mirror, that she will always carry her family with her. Many girls fondly look back on the boldness that allowed them to dance wildly, explore endlessly, or become pirate queens. Other contributors find moments of abandon once more in the midst of change and turmoil. In her poetry, one young woman embraces passion and trust even as she is wracked with heartache. Another insists on taking in life freely, knowing that it will be both bitter and sweet.

The words and images in this chapter also depict many of the difficulties girls face as they move out of girlhood. With insight and courage they write about taking on new responsibilities and roles, and sometimes feeling alone as they move toward adulthood. As she bravely and sadly wonders about the hardship her dad has faced, a young woman tells her father that she is ready to take on some of the roles he played when she was a child. Another girl writes about being forced to leave her home in the bush in order to go to school — she is torn about leaving her parents and moving to a town where she is unable to follow the ways of living taught by her Cree ancestors. This same girl finds strength in knowing that she will someday pass on tradition and stories to her own children. In contrast, a few young women write about their battles with their parents and their need to leave in order to be able to grow. Some of the girls' struggles are internal — while they have grown in many ways, they still feel child-like inside.

These young women want to pass on what they have learned. Even as they experience a vast array of emotions and insecurities, they want the world to know that they are capable and resilient. Collectively the pieces encourage girls to find the strength to accept themselves, to be okay with not being okay, to reach out in order to heal, to defy the concept of "normal." They tell other girls to seek out freedom, think critically, and love wholly. Their hopes are wide — *we will continue to learn and become. We will look to tradition and then we will make our own way. When we feel small and alone, we will lean on others or ourselves. We are talented and wise. And we believe in ourselves.*

*Girlhood is the time when you grow the most, it's the time when you can feel your lips smiling and your heart breaking. It's a time. You make it what you make it.*

JULIA C. REES, 16

# October 22nd

The day I knew we were all very much the same. The day I found razor blades in my basement and a few seconds later threw them away. The stormy night my mother gave me a poem she wrote about rain.

And when I paint my nails on the floor of my ugly carpeted bedroom, I remind myself of my aunt Jamie that summer time five years ago, in the old house. When we would sit cross-legged in the light that cast across the room from the setting sun. Our windows open all day and all night and the wind would make my bedroom door shut by itself. And every time my bedroom door shut by itself I would hear wind chimes coming from the patio downstairs. I'd see a light go on in the kitchen when I leaned over the railing of the loft bed my dad built me. I'd feel a breeze brush against my bed sheets and it would greet me with the smell of chimney smoke — reminding me of how much I love summer.

Today is the day I looked in the mirror and I saw my sisters, my mom and my dad.

EMMA RUTH, 15

a loss of innocence
ear piercings and
faerie wings (that glittered)
whyte ave afternoons
greasy spoon cafe lunches and
insomniac-writer's-block-nights
## learning how to be alone
(but not lonely)

sixteen was
a kaleidoscope of neon color
campfire songs at the river and
the brilliance of dr. seuss
waking up to see the sunrise
and crying so hard
i thought i would drown

sixteen was
a time of firsts:
first love
first boyfriend
first kiss behind a pop machine
at the calgary train station
first time i was convinced
that i would die for someone
(five people)
(my sisters)

sixteen was
a time of mistakes
learning that love
isn't always what you think it is
and sometimes
friends will lie
and boyfriends will cheat
but best friends (sisters)
will never leave

sixteen was
lots of loving
learning that family
isn't always the people
who are related to you
laughing too loud at 4 a.m.
iron-on t-shirts
and ouija board games
late at night

sixteen was
a time of laughter and
holding hands while singing
"we are all innocent"
and realizing
we really are innocent
there is something to live for
and that is right now

# Sixteen

ERIN LORENZ, 16

145

# I Grew Up

I grew among lights
in the buzzing land of the busy,
black umbrellas turning their backs
on rain and crowded alleys

I grew up with cars
and factory chimneys spewing
smoke like
ripe cigarettes

And the television arguing
with the radio over
nonsensical issues that
supposedly affect me

I grew with the river,
summer days spent plucking snails
off moist leaves
holding annual caterpillar circuses

And while searching avidly for grass-
hoppers
with hair like the wind,
knowing that there is no such thing
as a day

I grew up with the sun
and the stars and the moon,
bright eyes watching me from
the vastness of the universe

I grew in two places at once
intertwined

ANNA DZIUBA, 17

146

# Plants, Sky and Me

It was a desire to be free that inspired me to create my self-portrait.

CLARA
CHANG, 15

# My Stages Have Holes

I don't want to grow up. But only so much can be done to stop or control change. Over the years, I've watched the older girls' eagerness to grow up. Drawing all over their faces with eyeliner and lipstick, buying revealing clothes long before there was anything to reveal. Touching the arms of their male classmates, hoping to find that "spark" that even they couldn't explain. They hunted it — starved for attention. Call me crazy, but way back then, I was still more interested in kicking boys than kissing them, lipstick was for leaving messages on the bathroom mirror, and my birthday cakes were shaped like dinosaurs.

I miss the age when being friends with a guy meant just that. There were no 'what-ifs', no spin the bottle, and no lousy rumour mill. A time when smacking a guy wasn't flirting, and kissing was nothing more than a last-resort for revenge. Back then things were simple.

More and more though, I do want to look older, and everyday I am appalled to see more and more make-up on my face. My style is more provocative than it used to be, and I have developed a fascination with the "spark". Some days I feel like I've become my own worst enemy.

There's only so much stock I can place in the idea that "growing up" will solve all of my problems. That if I just start wearing a lot of make-up and stop acting wild — that I'll be "normal", well-adjusted, happy, mature... and attached. But I know better — nothing is that easy. And anyway, I'm not normal. I never wanted to be. And that's okay with me.

KILEY CROSSBY, 16

# getting out of this place

I can't keep my feet rooted
to the same old comfortable ground
I've got to resist this instinct
to curl up on the same couch, the same nest
where I'm growing up
these small town kids are getting restless
turning an agricultural fair into a riot
300 kids screaming 'Fuck the police!'
no one knew what quite to believe
when thirteen-year-old punks got arrested for possession
and wannabe thugs busted for tearing down white picket fences
all because there was nothing better to do
so feet trampled, rubber bullets flew
the cops were grateful to put their clubs to use
and everyone cheered when we made the news

ADÈLE BARCLAY, 18

*It isn't easy, being near adulthood yet barely out of childhood. Teen girls have so much to say and share with the world. We're all very capable and talented, and should be encouraged to pursue our passions, not chase after others' expectations.*

ANONYMOUS, 15

# Untitled

HEATHER KIM, 16

# Old Days

Remember the days
when we climbed the jungle gym
and visited all the world
in our cotton dresses
and scabby knees
I was a ruthless pirate queen
and you were the skipper brave
You were the ultimate rock star
I was your biggest groupie
I was your hero, and sure
you were the damsel in distress
We saw it all
and did it all
together as a team
We experienced life's ups
and laughed off all the downs
Now I stand
in my gorgeous prom dress
My knees have long since healed
I scan the crowd
wondering where you are
Are you still climbing jungle gyms
in cotton dresses and scabby knees?
Back in the old days

HEATHER ROBBINS, 14

# I Can

It won't be long now
This has been a long journey
But it'll be worth it in the end

I've been given a second chance
Everyday I await your arrival
Little one
You've given me hope
You've given me a reason to try

I know that I love you
That you've changed my life
When you move I feel a sense of security
Knowing that you're alive and okay
I can't wait to hold you or hear your first cry

As you learn from me I'll learn from you

*Justine is 6 weeks old now. Everyday I have challenges to face but there is no other place that I would rather be except right here with my little girl — she is my world. There is so much to say.*

ANNE MARIE, 16

## Teen Haiku

Rebellious teens
Brave, unique, and confident
Hope for the future

CHRISTINE LOH, 16

# Dance

It was best when the floor was cold and bare
We would twirl and float
like ice dancers across a smooth surface
Except our surface wasn't that smooth
and we didn't have that much space

We performed for crowds
of two, or three, or four,
but rarely could we see them
because we never could see that well
while we twirled

We often fell
and things were broken
or dresses ripped
but no one could tell us to stop
Because we would never let them

We danced to music that couldn't be heard
but only seen in our feet as they skipped
across the hardwood floors
Under the tables
Out of the room

RACHEL WELLMAN, 17

## Finding the Pieces

I was almost two years old when they finally signed the adoption papers, old enough to understand that my Mommy was giving me away and that I wouldn't see her anymore. As I got older, my Mom and Dad answered all my questions about my adoption. And I certainly had a lot. Who was my birth mother? Who was my birth father? Why did my mother give me up? What did I do wrong? They answered me the best they could, always honest. I never doubted for a moment that they loved me — not at all. Throughout my childhood, I continued to see my biological grandmother. I would stay the night at her apartment, and she would paint my toenails bright red and read me stories. Then we'd drive around in her white convertible, going to garage sales. I loved my Gramma.

When I was little, I was diagnosed with ADD, ADHD, ODD and was assigned two codes, 80 and 42. I was bright but my behaviour was a huge problem. I began to throw tantrums, and my Mom still jokes that one of my first full sentences was probably "No, you CAN'T make me! I won't!" My parents tried everything to help me. I went to my first psychologist around the age of four, and I proceeded to visit psychiatrists and counselors for years. I was put on medications — Dexitrin, Ritalin, Zoloft, Prozac. And things just kept getting more difficult. I was out of control. I threw tantrums, beat my head on walls, tore out my hair. Self-mutilation got me the attention I craved.

When I was in grade six, my Gramma died. I had lots of support dealing with her death, but it was never enough. My only blood relative was lost to me. My fun-loving, eccentric, funky Gramma was gone.

In high school I began to drink, smoke weed, and sneak out of the house at night to party with friends. I included my Mom and Dad less and less in my life, until I shut them out entirely. My whole life became a big lie. I was an actress all day. At school I was a popular girl, loved by many and hated by lots. I got kicked out of class more and more and was eventually suspended. I began engaging in sexual activities I wasn't ready for. Kids at school started calling me a whore. I slowly lost most of my friends, except for one. She knew everything that I did and I knew everything about her. We never even liked each other that much, but we had something in common. We were both self destructive and really mixed-up girls. We were making all the wrong choices, and we depended on each other to say it was alright, that we'd be okay.

Things at home came to a breaking point when my parents found out that I'd been sneaking out every night to be with my boyfriend. Even though I treated them like shit, I still loved my Mom and Dad, and disappointing them made my heart ache. I decided I couldn't take it — I couldn't live at home anymore. I told them I hated them, and that there was no way I was staying in their house any longer. My aunt and uncle decided to take me in and help me get on my feet. Once on the plane, I didn't look back. I pushed all my emotions aside until I was numb.

Things went well for six months, and then I began to fall back into that old pattern of getting myself in trouble. I started getting in fights at school, and I was suspended numerous times before I was expelled. I eventually started school at a program for adolescent girls at risk, and a month and a half later I'm still here.

I miss my family a lot, but I'm not quite ready to move back yet. I still have some things I need to do for myself and I still have some issues to work on. I get stuck in a rut sometimes and I still get in trouble. But I am working so hard to change, to find out who I am inside and to become that person. I'm happier than I've ever been.

I still wonder about my birth mother. Who is she? Where is she now? Does she think about me? Does she miss me? Does she regret giving me up? Someday maybe I'll meet her and I'll have one more person in my life that I can look to for some answers. Thinking back, I see now that it wasn't her fault. I know she loved me.

Life is full of unanswered questions. As soon as you get the answer to one question another one comes along. I still don't know who I am inside, but that's part of my journey. Everyday I learn more about myself and more about those around me. I don't have any regrets, none at all. I've learned something from every person I've met, from every mistake I've made. My life is a puzzle. I need to find all the pieces, including the unexpected and the ones that don't belong. There will always be room to add more pieces, to expand and learn and grow.

ANONYMOUS, 15

# Untitled

DECEMBER STORM, 13

# Birthday Letter

Dear Mom,

I sometimes don't like you and I sometimes think you don't like me. I rarely ever see you and I really don't think you care. I know we're going to have more fights, more screams, more tears.

But I want you to know that when you're gray and old I'll hold you, brush your hair, cry you to sleep. I'll be there because I love you. And even you can't change that.

Leah

*"I am sending you this letter on behalf of my daughter because she wouldn't be likely to submit it herself. I think it reveals what she and I are all about. She gave it to me on my birthday and wrote it that same day last October."*
*- Colleen Innes*

LEAH INNES, 15

# the beauty of it

Like every sixteen-year-old girl I was in love. I had met the boy of my dreams and I was surely going to be happy ever after. Our relationship lasted longer than the average high school romance. The ending, however, was blunt and far from painless. With a few of his words I was suddenly full of insecurity and doubt. I looked him in the eye and said, 'I forgive you'. Perhaps it was just a desperate plea for the perfect universe I had moments before.

But my story doesn't end there, or perhaps it didn't begin there. Weeks before, my sister and I had caught my mom in a lie. It wouldn't have hurt so bad, being cheated on, if I hadn't witnessed the pain it had caused my dad. My mom had an affair and we were the ones that had to tell him. My dad is my hero. At the time, I cried on the shoulder of my better-than-perfect beau who surely could never be capable of inflicting such pain on me. But a month later he left me and I went from being in love and living with my happy family, to living in a new home with a broken hearted dad as lonely hearted as me. I lost my school, my friends, my job, my boyfriend and my mom. I felt broken from the inside out. I drove my car down the highway with tears burning my cheeks and asked — where was God, why wasn't God doing anything to help me? And then I wondered if it was fair for me to blame God. I stopped waiting for God to answer me — I don't mind being a work in progress.

All of this has taught me to accept change. I've become okay with not being okay. I am ready for better things. My faith keeps me strong, and I've learned that life is about becoming. I've learned that hatred involves as much passion and dedication as love. I will not waste my time hating when inside I so badly want to love. I'm going to drink life as it presents itself, both the bitter and the sweet. The beauty of it is, the cup I choose to drink from is over-flowing.

NIKAYLA MCIVER, 17

*Being a teenage girl is not as easy as everyone thinks. So much is expected of us. We worry about our futures and long for the past. But we are generally pretty resilient. We'll find a way.*

JULIA MASTRANGELO, 15

## Every Step

I am trying to forgive you, and love you,
but how can I love someone
who constantly makes me feel like I am nothing?
every step forward means two steps back.
All I've ever wanted is a mother who loved me,
who I could talk to,
who wouldn't criticize or condemn my every action.
I am a strong, beautiful, independent young woman
and I am a crying child.

JENN RYAN, 17

164

# Ka Oopad Adums

When I was little I believed a story that my dad told me to keep me safe. I know the story is not true but I still believe it a little bit. I believe it because I believe in the old ways of living on the land. My dad told me the story because he wanted me to stay in the house at night so I wouldn't get hurt or lost. It worked.

*Listen…*

*Long ago, a shwayko lived by herself in the bush at Wakungi. One morning she woke up and heard a puppy crying at her door. She opened the door and brought it into her cabin. The puppy had wings so the shwayko called him Ka Oopad Adums, the flying dog. She loved him very much and he loved her.*

*When Ka Oopad Adums got older the shwayko was shocked to see him put his wings to use by flying. At night, Ka Oopad Adums would fly around, stealing people's food. The people became angry with the shwayko because Ka Oopad Adums was stealing their food. So the shwayko killed Ka Oopad Adums.*

*But the next morning Ka Oopad Adums came back to the cabin and the shwayko became scared. She locked the window and wouldn't let him in. Every morning the dog came back and scratched on her window. So, the shwayko decided to move away to a place where Ka Oopad Adums couldn't find her. But he did find her and when he did the shwayko disappeared. Years later the shwayko's clothes were found.*

'Shwayko' is a Cree word that means 'woman'.

*They had been ripped by a dog and had blood on them. People still hear Ka Oopad Adums flying around. They say he's looking for someone to take care of him.*

That is the story of Ka Oopad Adums that I was told as a child. I've never seen him because he's a spirit, a ghost. But I did hear him flying one night when I was out in the canoe with my dad. I've been told that if he catches you he'll kill you. And they'll only find your clothes.

It can be confusing because I know my parents told me this story to keep me home and keep me safe, but sometimes I think that I should live in town. I don't know what to do or how I'm going to figure it out. It's hard right now, being a teenage girl, because I have to go to school and that means I can't live with my parents. I like to help my mom cook and sew, dress caribou and moose, prepare geese. Often I just dream of living far away in the bush.

The story of Ka Oopad Adums is important to me because it's part of my past. My dad told the story to me, my grandfather told the story to my father, and my great-grandfather to my grandfather. When I am a mother I'm going to tell this same story to my children.

ELIZABETH MIANSCUM, 14

# Blue

Another December day
I can't sleep
to dream these walls away
wrapped in my blanket
like the kid I used to be
Sunshine you called me
I can't count the times
we laughed until you cried
Who keeps track anyway?

And the nights spent all alone
work all day
Say *I love you* on the telephone
What I wouldn't give
to rub your tired feet
and watch tv until we fall asleep
home

Such sentimentality —
nintendo days
and our three foot christmas tree
My eyes hold

a tribute to the past
Eighteen years
and I still can't believe
how much I see of you in me

So much to say and do
I want the rain to come
and paint me a different shade
of blue

I am so small
beneath my blanket
my eyes close
knowing I will see you soon


TERRI PROKOPIW, 19

# Untitled

YALDA A., 19

# Daddy Poem

I seldom see your face anymore
you're always turned away into books or asleep or
getting into cars and going places.

These days have been sad.
I go to work with my music on and
speed away from this house, these walls that crumble
a little more with each minute, each day
that slips away from our growing ups
together.

When your mother died
I had nothing to do but carry on,
but did you carry on?
Into those rooms
where she had killed the spiders for you
now filled with dusty webs.

And what about me?
Can I still wake you up
to get a mouse out of the trap?
There are so many spiders
in the rooms of my new life
and I'm still scared.

Sometimes I can't get off the phone with you
you're so distant I fill the
space with words about my day
or my friends and you just
listen.

But what can I give you?
I have no more days left as a child

and yet so many spiders.
When she was sick
you were the only one there to help her eat
chocolates.
We were too young and too scared to understand
how painful it must have been
to watch her struggle with the hard-shelled ones,
how she would break every bone
just to eat a chocolate
just to prove she was still alive
and now eating a chocolate is like flying a flag of life
amongst the skin and bones
of death and memory.

And it would have been so much easier
to set traps that would kill them,
finish their tiny lives,
let you sleep at night.
But you kept them alive for us,
sacrificed sleep and patience
so we could stay warm in bed
and dream our dreams.
That's what you've been doing —
keeping the world alive for us.
You must be so tired.

Let me kill the spiders for you, daddy.
I'll take out the mouse this time.
And while you sleep,
I'll clear these rooms of dusty webs
and let you dream
your own dreams.

KAITLIN SCHWAN, 18

# Growing

The creator made me.

As a child I grew
    to have courage
    to have wisdom
    to be strong.

I am growing in so many ways,
and still I am a child at heart.

ANONYMOUS, 18

# Mi Reflejo

THALIA C. ANTONIO SOTO, 17

*"I wrote this during my last week as a patient at a day-treatment program for eating disorders. It is a treasure chest of what I learned."*

# Splendors

I sing that your clothes should fit you, that you should not have to fit your clothes.

I sing knowing that you're not alone. Share and be open with others, and you will be surprised how fast you will heal.

I sing that you will not waste your time looking in the mirror. It is a piece of glass, with edges so sharp it can rip you apart. Life is better spent enjoying the splendors that surround us, rather than picking apart the marvels we wish were not ours.

I sing not wasting your time on jealousy.

I sing that you are not worthless. I sing you're a good person who deserves goodness. What life gives you may not be ok and that is normal.

I sing because someone loves you.

I sing not reading beauty magazines. I sing your sense of beauty, which is independent of two-dimensional glossy images. If you decide to read beauty magazines, I sing to indulge with a critical mind.

I sing getting to know your parents because time is ticking and they may be gone soon — today, tomorrow, next year. I sing giving them a chance. They just might surprise you at how insightful they are.

I sing not forgetting to smile. Your smile is the first thing that people will notice about you. I sing how amazing it is that seventeen tiny little muscles can brighten a day.

I sing creating solutions.

# I sing because I believe in you.

JESSICA SHEWBRIDGE, 16

# embracing myself

As I grow up, I'm learning about the importance of accepting myself. Instead of becoming angry and frustrated with myself when I'm upset, I try to tell myself that it is perfectly okay to be sad sometimes. I need to embrace, accept, encourage, and recognize all the different parts of me. As young women, we need a strong sense of ourselves in order to cope with media images that tell us how we should be. We start believing that we should hate ourselves — when what we really need to know is that how we look, how we feel, and how we are right now is absolutely fine.

LIZ TOOHEY-WIESE, 16

# conclusion
of the book, not the story

*Girls...*
'*I want to tell you how much I admire you. I want to tell you to have courage, to resist, to fight back where my generation has not and to do it with joy and creativity. I want to tell you how fabulous you are, how good, what wonders await you. I want to encourage you to be unafraid, to write, to tell — and when you fall, to fall forward. I want to tell you to organize, become politicized, analyze, make a lot of noise, dance and have fun. I want you to forgive us where we have failed, teach us and learn with us.*'
— *Jane Doe (writer, teacher, feminist activist)*

In publishing this book, we wanted to bring the creative voices of girls and young women to the forefront in order to elicit awareness and action, and also to bring hope to those girls who feel alone. We know we aren't the only ones who care about the well being of young women. We hope that, through this book, the creative works of our contributors will help to bring about change. Change can come from increased awareness, critical thinking, or concrete action.

On these pages and the few that follow, we offer up the words and wisdom of women twenty years and older. We asked women (including ourselves) what we would say to girls across Canada if given the chance. These messages reveal some of what we wish we'd been told during our teenage years and send the word out to girls and young women that they are not alone. We applaud girls' beauty, resilience, and intelligence — and tell them again, you are '*brighter, louder, and stronger*' than others have told you.

**Untitled 1**

'I want to tell you to share your feelings, fears, and worries with those you love and trust — even if it seems a bit scary. I bet you'll be surprised to find out that others share some of those same feelings. It's likely that they will hear parts of themselves in your voice and will become inspired to share their stories too. It's comforting to know that we're not alone.'

– Michelle Clarke (photographer)

**Untitled 2**

*'You can create change. When you feel passionate about something in your life, just go for it. Speak out. Take action. It's okay to make mistakes along the way — you will learn and grow from the experience.'*

*– Michelle Clarke (photographer)*

Our contributors have spoken from places of struggle and spaces of heartache, from feelings of inspiration and moments of joy. Girls' exploration of their identities resound with honesty, and their voices are undeniably clear, intelligent, honest, and captivating. It takes great courage to come forward and tell stories of loneliness, hardship, and struggle — many of these young women have drawn on their learning and strength in order to share some of their most vulnerable moments.

'Feminism isn't about conforming to a new set of rules. It's not about telling yourself or others what to think. It's not about what you wear or who you think is hot. It's not about the music you listen to or the books you read. Feminism is a tool for you to connect with generations of women who've been through some incredible things and accomplished some amazing changes in this world and who've thought some incredible thoughts. Pick it up and use it to make something true and beautiful and strong – just like you.'
– Lisa Rundle (co-editor of Turbo Chicks: Talking Young Feminisms)

'I wish that, when I was a little girl, I had more adult women to help direct my path. When I was 13 and thought that friends were the only ones that mattered, I wish my mother had told me that family is important because you only have your parents for a little while longer. When I was 16, I wish my older sister had told me that trying to exchange sex for love would not make me secure or happy. When I was 19, I wish my teacher had told me that education would open many doors to the dreams that seemed impossible — and that with education, my colour would be less of a barrier to those hard-to-enter professions. I wish all of the women in my life had realized how important it was to pour into me with their support and guidance. Now that I am a mother, I promise to tell my daughter and all you girls, you are beautiful, you are smart...and you are loved!'
– Natasha Burford (mother and friend)

Some are outraged, and with outrage comes demands for change. Others hope that girls will be able to find comfort in their words and images. Many of the works reach into places of despair and then reveal the power of wit and humor as a source of sustenance. As they embrace calmness and exuberance, laughter and light, girls and young women have also captured what it is about girlhood that makes them soar. Their self-awareness and insight hold lessons for us all.

*'That feeling — the one that gets you in the gut and makes you feel so alone and scared and strange — that feeling you get when you watch your friends walk away when you need them to stay, or when you are compared with someone or something that you can never be, or when you do something that you know betrays your own self — you're not alone. Others have that feeling, and rather than treating each other badly, or treating yourself badly, it is so worth it to be kind. Be kind to yourself. Know that you are worth kindness.'*
*– Beth Pentney*
*(student and feminist)*

We hope that you will take with you the messages in *Voice* that tell us — every one of us — to accept girls and young women for who they are. Their works remind us to let them develop in their own unique ways (complications and contradictions included), to embrace their individuality, to never judge and *never* underestimate them. They are asking for support as they defy the messages they receive about *how* they should act or *who* they should be. And they are telling us to give them the space to grow and change, and then to reach out, listen, accept, and love.

*Beauty* holds reminders that girls are fully aware of the contradictions in the messages they receive about their bodies, their looks, and their place in the world. Many of the pieces express the fragility of girls and young women as they enter into the realms

> 'Be strong in yourself. Don't take crap from anyone — but also remember to find the courage to look within and decide if there may be a bit of truth in it. You are unique; no one else in the world is like you. You are not fat, ugly or dumb. You are bodacious, beautiful and brilliant. Believe in yourself, there are millions of us who have passed through your journey before you that believe in you. You are never alone.'
> — Vicky Green (a woman with a wee bit of wisdom and a wisp of grey hair)

of beauty and desire. These works can act as reminders that oppressive messages about their bodies abound — girls need spaces where they can articulate their anger and challenge stereotypes. This section is also a place where young women have expressed their excitement and anticipation, hesitancy, and spontaneity, as they explore desire. With support and trust, they will enter into love, navigate through heartache, and sing with passion.

*Strength* is a call for compassion, resilience, and action. These girls and young women have spoken out about racism, exclusion, abuse, rape, and violence. They have written about addiction and depression. Some of them discuss their ways of coping as they move through anguish. With striking intensity, many point to the continued need for women and girls to come together, share insights and support one another as we break through barriers. They are telling us, our collective work is not yet done.

The message that *Becoming* offers is one of finding acceptance for ourselves and each other as we travel through adolescence and beyond. The girls and young women in this chapter explore the complications and determination of family. They look back with tenderness at the passing of childhood, embrace the exhilarating moments of girlhood, and make tentative steps toward their futures.

These works are a gentle reminder of the importance of witnessing each other's sorrow, believing in ourselves, and leaning on each other as we move forward.

The voices of the girls and young women in this book

> *'When I was a teenager I thought my life would start at some pre-set age, say, 21. Adolescence felt like a long painful waiting period I had to endure until my real life started. What I wish I had known is that life is not some static thing you arrive at, it's a constant work in progress. My life is no more real at 28 than at 16 — I just have different choices. So try to have patience with yourself, and with your life. Make the most of the choices that you have today.'*
> *— Rachel Sutton (midwifery student)*

are holding up a light to the truths in their lives. *You've heard some of what we have to say and you've witnessed some of what we need to show. You've seen our strength, and glimpsed a sense of ourselves. Hold on to what we've given. Carry our stories with you.*

*Girls, we want you to know that we see you, all that you are and all that you are becoming.* We hope you see yourselves, all you are and all you are becoming. *You are poised at an interesting point in time — girls and young women have never had so many rich opportunities, have never had so many new doors open. At the same time, your struggles are also unique from those that girls and young women have faced in decades past. Many of you are rising to meet these struggles head on by challenging what you are told about who you should be. You are being gender rebellious in such a good way, by resisting definitions of girlhood and womanhood that constrict and constrain. Keep it up and join with others. Continue to tell your stories, write honestly, dance hard, sing strong, and paint wildly. Trust yourselves.*

*– Jessica Hein, Heather Holland, Carol Kauppi*

# a closer look
## grounding girls' voices in a feminist approach

If you would like to learn more about girlhood and the *GirlSpoken* project, read on for details. This chapter provides information about the background to the project, submissions to the book, a snapshot of our contributors, our survey and the other activities related to the book project and the user-guide that is available to accompany the book.

*Girlhood and the Feminist Landscape*
The primary focus of the *GirlSpoken* project is to foster self-expression and growth among girls and young women. It was developed as an action project to establish new community-based programming for girls, and also as a university-based research project. We recognized that there were gaps in the theoretical understanding of girls' experiences and perspectives, and wanted to broaden the ways in which girlhood is perceived. We wanted to learn from girls and young women, through a participatory action project that involved them in many activities. This desire is partly informed by the idea of the *otherness* of childhood and girlhood, which recognizes that the lived worlds of girls differ from those of adult women.[1] To understand their lived realities, we must gather their stories, listen, and learn from them. While the area of girls' studies has been developing rapidly since 2000, knowledge in this area has been somewhat limited by the notion that girls' studies is a distraction from the "real" work of addressing the larger political and economic problems linked to gender inequality. The recent

publication of two scholarly books on girlhood has strengthened this area of critical thought[2].

Yet much remains to be accomplished; changing the prevalent ways of viewing adolescence and girlhood is slow and arduous. There is no shortage of theories on adolescence that depict young people as a problem[3]. Early theories were based on the idea that turmoil and stress were the main features of the teenage years, due to the physical changes and surging hormones associated with this stage of life. In disputing this view, other writers have shifted the emphasis to risks, individuation, or social factors, to name a few approaches. More recently, women writers and researchers have called into question the prevailing understandings of the teenage years, especially in the way they represent girls. Girls and women have often been depicted as being weak and fragile, confined to restricted modes of femininity and separated from traits and behaviors defined as male. Another persistent problem is that developmental theories on girlhood generally assume heterosexuality.[4]

Feminist work has inspired new questions about girlhood. This work challenges the overly simplified portrayal of girls as passively accepting definitions of gender. New knowledge about girls shows how many resist negative and restrictive aspects of traditional femininity and engage in forms of "gender rebellion"[5]. Such writing for and about girls focuses on their perspectives and stories as a way to learn how they are creating new modes of femininity. The *GirlSpoken* project was inspired by this approach to learning about girls' lives.

We developed a project to explore girls' and young women's understandings of identity and what it means to be a teenage girl in Canada. In the call for submissions for this book, we asked girls, "what makes you who you are?" and "what do you want to tell the world about what it's like to be you?" Identity speaks to a central aspect of girlhood that reveals how individual girls are connected to wider historical and social contexts. Notions of selfhood do not develop solely through internal, mental processes of discovery. Rather, the self is produced — socially constructed — through interactions with the world. We are all classified, coded, named, disciplined, and regulated by others.[6] This process of classification is linked to long-standing ideas about aspects such as gender, sexuality, race, class, and ability. How girls speak of their identities can reveal much about how they have come to know themselves through their interactions with others and the worlds they inhabit. While identity reflects the nature of power relations in a girl's life, it also reflects struggle and resistance. Gathering girls' stories of identity is a potent way to explore how they are resisting forces of classification and regulation as a means of gaining a sense of control.

This book, offering reflections of girls' identities, is the result of four years of work. We approached the subject matter from several angles: we gathered and shared information through workshops, interviews, a survey, a traveling exhibit of creative works by girls, and the call for creative submissions by Canadian girls that culminated in this book. With funding from the Ontario Trillium Foundation, the multi-year project began in 2002.

### The *GirlSpoken* Project

We created the project to respond to a gap in information and resources by, for, and about teenage girls between the ages of thirteen and nineteen. The main goal of *GirlSpoken* is to provide forums for girls to express themselves creatively and to connect with other girls. Our aim was to understand how forms of creative self-expression can support girls in exploring critical issues in their lives, understanding how gender matters in their lives, and building confidence and self-esteem. We wanted to use an approach that included girls and young women in a wide range of activities based on feminist principles and values. Introducing girls to language and discussion that allow them to name experiences of injustice is empowering. By doing this, we hoped to allow new, relevant knowledge to emerge about girlhood. But a challenge to using this approach stems from concerns that many girls and young women shy away from a connection with feminism. This is largely due to the influence of dominant discourses which teach girls that progress has been made, that gender discrimination has ended, and that feminism is a taboo[7]. Even though girls often accept feminist principles and values, this does not mean that they are ready to confront the underlying sexism in their lives by joining a feminist program. In focussing attention on creative activities, but also grounding the *GirlSpoken* project on feminist principles and practices, girls were attracted to the project. We incorporated several feminist principles and practices into the *GirlSpoken* activities and, in the section that follows, we explain how these principles guided the book project.

*Recognizing that young women are experts on their own lives*
The principle of understanding girls' perspectives and lived realities informed all of our project activities. Believing in the importance of exploring strengths as a means of building confidence and developing a proud sense of self, we involved girls in an advisory group to help with the selection process, and consulted our

participants about revisions to their creative works. In allowing girls to speak for themselves, through their writing and art pieces, rather than through our interpretation of them, knowledge gained from this book can validate girls' lives and experiences.

*Striving for accessibility and diversity*
Naming the interconnected forms of oppression that women and girls face is essential. The research activities explored issues of diversity and *GirlSpoken* developed programs and materials, including this book, that aim to be inclusive and anti-oppressive with regards to sexual identity, gender identity, body size, class, ability, religion, racial identity, culture, and ethnic background. Feminist standpoint theory draws attention to the importance of girls' social locations and how their location in society gives prominence to certain aspects of their lives while obscuring others. We wanted to gather and share information from the standpoints of girls in various social locations, and to include those in the book who experience a different reality from dominant or mainstream groups. For example, in the call for proposals and the selection process for the book, we tried to reach out specifically for submissions from various minority cultural groups, queer and transgendered youth, girls in group homes, and girls of differing abilities, to mention just a few. We also recognize that, regardless of how effective and inclusive our outreach may have been, we were still soliciting work in an oppressive culture. Girls' experiences with oppression and their differing social supports mean that some girls are much less likely to value their own voices and are thus less likely to express themselves in public forums (e.g., through a response to our call for submissions).

*Making the link between creative expression, learning and self-esteem*
*GirlSpoken* takes the view that the process of engaging in arts-based activities is more important than what is produced. Arts-based activities act as a tool for self-exploration and group learning. By exhibiting and publishing girls' work, we have aimed to build confidence among contributors and decrease isolation amongst readers. This book, and the exhibit based on the pieces in it, are meant to employ art as a tool to spark constructive discussion on issues of importance to girls.

*Developing youth-driven initiatives*
Girls, on the whole, have little power in our society. As a project seeking to build understanding about girlhood, *GirlSpoken* is strongly committed to conducting activities in a way that is empowering. We involved young women in the development, decision making, and implementation of many of the project activities leading to the call for submissions and in the selection process for the book. The content of this book is a response to girls' needs, as voiced by girls, through feedback from a girls' advisory group, our workshop participants, and girls who participated in our interviews and our survey. In publishing this book, we have sought to create a space for girls to speak for themselves through their writing and art.

*Using a holistic approach*
We have used a holistic approach to understanding girls' lives. We began the project by conducting individual interviews and workshops with girls and then used this information to develop and refine the other project activities. This book is part of the broader aim of *GirlSpoken* to produce progressive resources for girls, based on

work by girls. Our holistic approach strives to reveal the multitude of interconnected challenges that girls face in adolescence, and the pieces in this book help to bring those challenges to light.

*Developing collaborative relationships*
We have been working with many different individuals and groups in order to fulfill our goal of carrying out project activities. Our efforts have been greatly rewarded as women (and some men) in all parts of the country have promoted the project activities related to this book. Our success has depended on a cooperative approach in which individuals and organizations worked together.

Based on these principles, *GirlSpoken* has developed new programming for girls in the form of arts-based workshops, conducted research activities, and shared girls' experiences and stories through traveling exhibits, our website and this book. In the next few pages, you will find further information about these project activities.

**Call for Creative Submissions**
In the Fall of 2004, we broadcast a national call for creative submissions by teenage girls under age twenty, inviting them to send us non-fictional pieces on the theme of identity. Using the post, fax, and e-mail, we sent posters to schools and organizations serving girls and young women. The call for submissions asked girls to speak their minds and express how their backgrounds and experiences have shaped who they are. The poster informed them of how they could share their experiences of growing up as part of the *GirlSpoken* anthology of creative writing and artwork. Educators and service providers distributed the information to

potential contributors. Submissions arrived daily for several months. In total, we received over 800 pieces, mainly in the form of poetry, prose, diary entries, drawings, paintings, photographs, and collages. Reflecting the broad distribution of the poster campaign, the submissions came from teenage girls living in all parts of Canada.

## The Selection Process

Our selection process was guided by the desire to include the varied perspectives and multiple experiences of teenage girls in Canada, while also creating a book that speaks strongly to their interests, passions, struggles, and successes. Making decisions about which pieces to include was challenging — even agonizing at times. Recognizing the popularity of zines and blogs that offer girls uncensored forms of self-expression, our goal was to create something similar in a book. Choosing not to censor can be risky though, and we realize that some

writing and artwork in the book may provoke strong responses of approval or disapproval. We grappled with the question of whether it is appropriate to include or exclude a piece that reflects a contributor's internal struggle over the meaning of identity if there is some chance that it may offend another. In including controversial pieces, we hope that our readers will view them as opportunities for examining forms of oppression and "otherness," opening dialogue, and challenging divisions.

The results of our 2004 survey of 556 teenage girls in northern and southern Ontario gave us up-to-date information about areas of vital interest to teenage girls — topics and issues that speak to their current realities. The *GirlSpoken* survey showed that over half wanted to know more about girls' and women's issues, eating disorders or body image, health issues, and violence, and more than a third were interested in learning about specific topics such as leadership, health, GLBTQQ (gay, lesbian, bisexual, transgendered, queer and questioning) issues, schooling, poverty and homelessness, racism, harassment, and bullying. We wanted the book to include content on these issues as well as other topics that girls want to learn about.

In early 2005, *GirlSpoken* Coordinators Jess and Heather began the selection process to identify pieces for inclusion in the book. A goal was to include strong works that reflect the range of writing and artwork submitted to us and that address the interests of girls and young women. Young women attending the arts and writing program at a secondary school agreed to participate on a Selection Committee to help with the work of selecting poetry, prose, and artwork for the book. Four wonderfully perceptive, thoughtful and dedicated young women — Allison, Nina, Elena, and Jessica — offered their thoughts on the pieces and helped us to envision the book.

*Themes and Issues in the Book*

The art and writing in this book reveal the complex realities for Canadian girls and young women. The submissions cover varied topics and issues. Rather than organizing the book by discrete topics, we chose to focus on four general themes. We checked on our organization of the pieces in each chapter by using techniques of qualitative analysis to identify the unique elements in each chapter. In *Voice* the writing and artworks speak out strongly, especially about the ways in which gender matters, about restrictions, and countering them. *Beauty* deals with the challenges of navigating the shifting terrain between childhood and adolescence especially experiences associated with notions of beauty and sexuality, and questioning conventional categories based on gender. In *Strength*, girls expose forms of abuse, critique prevailing patriarchal traditions, and construct new femininities which show that girls and women have much to offer through forms of active resistance. In *Becoming*, girls recognize the importance of connections and belonging, even though pain and loss is sometimes part of the experience. *Becoming* is also about leaving childhood for adolescence or womanhood.

Some themes appear in more than one chapter. It may seem obvious that the central concept behind this book — identity — appears in every chapter. Girls reveal all sides of self-hood, including the destruction of self or efforts to hide their real selves in the face of serious difficulties such as abuse, bullying, harassment, or the loss of close relationships, as well as the joy of loving, liking or accepting themselves when they recognize their own strengths.

Some submissions in every chapter describe various forms of abuse, bullying, harassment, social exclusion, and marginalization. Gossip, the rumor mill, and whisper campaigns do not inflict physical wounds like rape and physical abuse, but these forms of bullying can cause deep emotional pain and scarring. In writing and artwork, some contributors confront their experiences of "otherness" and discrimination related to cultural background or race, physical differences, or sexuality.

One additional theme is strongly present in every chapter of the book — coping strategies and desires to make change. Our contributors share their ways of coping with challenges in their lives. While some coping strategies are destructive of self, such as cutting, eating disorders, or substance use, many girls describe the positive tactics they use to deal with circumstances in their lives. Some of these coping strategies involve a strong desire for making change in their worlds.

*A Snapshot of Our Contributors*
The contributors are Canadian girls of varied backgrounds and characteristics. The diversity among these girls and young women is reflected in their place of residence, age, cultural background, economic circumstances, and family characteristics. They include girls of differing abilities, heterosexual and queer girls, those writing from a place of privilege, and those who face adversity and oppression. In expressing ideas about identity, some contributors reveal their social locations, and many question assumptions about the expectations placed on girls and women, challenge the notion of gender defined as female and male, enjoy being gender rebellious, and generally convey the shifting, evolving and varying perspectives of Canadian girls.

The art and writing in the book is from girls in all regions of the country. The contributors were teenagers when they created their submissions and their average age was seventeen when they sent them to us. The girls reflect diverse cultural groups. Like other Canadian girls across the country, over half (57%) are Anglophone youth with ancestry from a wide range of European countries. A significant number of our contributors (about a quarter, at 24%) are members of various minority groups of Asian, African, Caribbean, and South or Central American roots. The contributors also include teens who describe themselves as French Canadians or Acadians (7%), Aboriginal or Métis (7%), and Jewish or Arabic (5%). Our contributors generally reflect the range of ethno-cultural backgrounds of Canadians but they include more participants from minority groups and slightly more Aboriginals, but fewer French Canadians. The relatively small number of French Canadians is likely because, unfortunately, the scope of this project did not allow us to gather submissions in both official languages and our call for submissions was in English.

It was our hope to include the voices of teenage girls from all social and economic groups and the contributors to the book are from all kinds of families. Most participants describe their families as having average or above-average income levels but a fifth are from low-income families. The parents of contributors are in a wide range of fields and occupations, such as professionals and mangers in health, law and teaching, artists, small business owners, tradespersons, and laborers, and they also include some who are unemployed.

The family structures and living circumstances of a number of contributors are reflected in their writing. Just over half (56%) of our contributors live with both parents. A few live with extended family members, typically grandparents or aunts and uncles.

Nearly a quarter (23%) are from single parent families and a small number live with a step-parent. A few contributors live in other circumstances — a group home, foster home, a boarding home, or on their own.

## The GirlSpoken Survey

We have used the survey results in the book to provide information on trends or patterns in girls' experiences. In the non-fictional creative works, girls tell us stories about their lives; the survey findings complement these stories by telling us how common or uncommon these experiences are among a large sample of teenage girls in Ontario.

In 2004, we conducted a survey of 556 teenage girls in small- and medium-sized communities in northern and southern Ontario. A goal was to gain a better understanding of the experiences and views of a large sample of teenage girls in Ontario. We developed the survey to reflect the issues identified by girls and young women in workshops and individual interviews. The questionnaire asked about girls' experiences on a wide range of topics including family, peers, school, body image, personal power, romance and sexuality, health, assertiveness, communication, harassment, bullying, abuse and conflict resolution, activities and interests, community involvement, and self-care.

The participants were girls and young women attending secondary schools. Most girls (542) completed the survey in their health or physical education classes but a small number (14) were clients of community-based services and they completed the questionnaire in the agency setting. A strength of the survey is that, in most instances, all girls in the class participated in the survey. This helped to build diversity into the sample. Our survey participants included girls from varied ethno-cultural groups, including Anglophones of European backgrounds, Francophones, Aboriginals and those from visible minority groups. However, the latter two groups were under-represented in the sample, compared with the Canadian population. The family structures and living circumstances of the survey participants were similar to those of the contributors to the book in that just over half (58%) were living with both parents. About a third of the survey participants were living in single parent families (14%) or in blended families (16%). A small number of the survey participants were living in other kinds of housing circumstances, similar to those of our contributors to the book (e.g. foster homes or group homes). According to Statistics Canada[8], a quarter of Canadian children and youth live in lone-parent families, so a smaller proportion of our survey participants were living in this type of family arrangement. However, a larger proportion of the girls in our survey were living in blended families compared to other Canadian children and youth. Although it has some limitations, the survey findings provide a good indication of the experiences and views of teenage girls.

### Arts-based Workshop Series

The goal of the *GirlSpoken* programming activities is to build self-confidence and self-esteem in girls so that they are better able to address the challenges they are facing in their lives. The *GirlSpoken* workshops are meant to create open spaces where girls can think, speak, explore, and create. Through discussion, brainstorming, and creative activities, girls are able to delve into the issues that are important to them, come up with solutions, and figure out new ways of being in the world. The art-based, five-week workshop series is focussed on the themes of identity, communication, body image, dating relationships, sexuality, and women's health. We have developed art activities that are suitable for everyone, regardless of their individual skills or abilities. Our approach is based on the idea that everyone can become an "artist" and that, through the creative process, new ideas and realizations are formed. *GirlSpoken* offered workshops in communities across northern and southern Ontario. In 2005, we partnered with Francophone and Aboriginal organizations in Sudbury, Ontario in order to adapt the *GirlSpoken* workshop guidelines to be culturally appropriate for use specifically with Francophone and Aboriginal girls. The Francophone workshop guidelines are entitled *Lignes directrices des ateliers filles fantastiques: Une approche artistique à la programmation pour les jeunes femmes.* All three versions of the workshop manual, including the original guidelines, as well as the adaptations for Francophone and Aboriginal girls, are available through the *GirlSpoken* website at www.girlspoken.com.

### Making Her Mark: A Traveling Exhibit

The traveling exhibit gave voice to the experiences, thoughts and ideas of girls and young women. It beckoned to audiences at conferences, galleries, and social service agencies to learn about the experiences and identities of girls and young women in Ontario. The exhibit toured across the province in 2004 and 2005. It explored girls' and young women's identities through their writings, collages, photos, and paintings. Various pieces explored body image, relationships, cultural identity, sexuality, racism, future goals and dreams, self-expression, political values, sexism, friendship, volunteering, creativity, the celebration of women's bodies, and much more. Submissions for *Making Her Mark* came from Peterborough, Thunder Bay, Toronto, Guelph, Kingston, the Six Nations Reserve of Grand River, Brantford, and Mount Hope. Future exhibits will include original artworks submitted for this book.

We believe that having the opportunity to participate in a traveling exhibit lets girls know that their voices matter and that they should be heard. Expressing their views and experiences, and participating in a province-wide or national-level project builds confidence and self-esteem in girls and young women. The exhibit also shares the experiences of the contributors with girls who are viewers. A girl who is struggling with body image can read about the experience of a girl who has overcome an eating disorder and who has come to love and accept her body. In this way, viewers can learn from other girls' experiences and feelings of isolation may be eased. *Making Her Mark* was interactive in that it invited viewers to become participants. We set up tables full of supplies for viewers to create their own works in response to the themes addressed in the exhibit. Girls who were viewers became active participants and continued the exploration of identity by contributing their own voices and experiences. The intent was to encourage them to pick up their own pens, brushes and pencils, and make marks of their own.

### Future Activities
The funding for *GirlSpoken* ended in 2005, but we have continued to work on the project though activities such as this book, and the creation of a new exhibit which opened at the Anna Leonowens Gallery at the Nova Scotia College of Art and Design in July, 2007. We continue to present the findings from the *GirlSpoken* research

activities and have produced a user-guide for this book. The guide outlines a wide range of learning and arts-based activities for girls. It is suitable for use by individuals and groups and uses the writing and art in this book as a springboard for readers to engage in discussion and their own self-expression. The user guide is useful for girls and young women, educators, service providers, and parents, guardians or other adults who want to explore this book through a guided tour. You can download the guide on the *GirlSpoken* website at www.girlspoken.com or on the Second Story Press website at www.secondstorypress.ca.

[1]Philo, C. (2003). 'To go back up the side hill': memories, imaginations and reveries of childhood. Children's Geographies, 1 (1), 7-23.

[2]Bettis, P. & Adams, N. (2005). Geographies of Girlhood: Identities In-between. Lawrence Erlbaum Associates. Jiwani, Y., Steenbergen, C & Mitchell, D. (2006). Girlhood: Redefining the Limits. Black Rose Books.

[3]Griffin, C. (1997). Representations of the young. In Roch, J. & Tucker, S., Youth in Society. London: SAGE Publications.

[4]Keefer, B. & Reene, K. (2002). Female adolescence: difficult for heterosexual girls, hazardous for lesbians. Annual Review of Psychoanalysis, 30, 245-252.

[5]Kelly, D., Pomerantz, S, & Currie, D. (2006). "No Boundaries"? Girls' interactive, online learning about femininities. Youth & Society, 38 (1), 3-38.

[6]Pini, M. (1997). Technologies of the self. In Roch, J. & Tucker, S., Youth in Society. London: SAGE Publications.

[7]Rowe-Finkbeiner, K. (2004). The F Word: Feminism in Jeopardy. Emeryville, CA: Seal Press.

[8]Statistics Canada. (2005). Census families in private households by family structure and presence of children (2001 Census). www40.statcan.ca/101/cst01/famil54b.htm

Centre Victoria pour femmes was our project partner in producing the French workshop guidelines.

Professor Cheryle Partridge, Native Human Services, Laurentian University took the lead role in working with Aboriginal organizations in Sudbury.